VIA LUCIS

Via Lucis

The Life of Jesus in the Light of Easter

Luis Antonio G. Cardinal Tagle

LITURGICAL PRESS
Collegeville, Minnesota
www.litpress.org

1 2 3 4 5 6 7 8 9

Library of Congress Cataloging-in-Publication Data

Names: Tagle, Luis Antonio, author.
Title: Via Lucis : the life of Jesus in the light of Easter / Luis Antonio G. Cardinal Tagle, DD, STD.
Description: Collegeville, Minnesota : Liturgical Press, 2017. | Originally published under title: Via Lucis : reflections in the Holy Land : Loyola Heights, Quezon City, Philippines : Jesuit Communications Foundation, Inc., c2016.
Identifiers: LCCN 2017028588 (print) | LCCN 2017051404 (ebook) | ISBN 9780814645420 (ebook) | ISBN 9780814645185
Subjects: LCSH: Holy Week—Meditations. | Jesus Christ—Biography—Passion Week. | Christian pilgrims and pilgrimages—Israel. | Israel—Description and travel. | Catholic Church—Prayers and devotions.
Classification: LCC BT414 (ebook) | LCC BT414 .T34 2017 (print) | DDC 232.9/01—dc23
LC record available at https://lccn.loc.gov/2017028588

Contents

Day Three

Day Four

Day Five

Day Six

Day Seven

Foreword

The pilgrimage to Jerusalem took place in 2011. It was a special journey for two reasons. First, our pilgrimage chaplain was no less than Luis Antonio Cardinal Tagle. He was just appointed Archbishop of Manila at that time. This was in fact his first time in the Holy City. He regarded it therefore as God's wonderful way of preparing him for his new, albeit challenging assignment. It was a treat for us, his companions, to witness this modern-day apostle of Christ take in the sights and sounds of Jerusalem, the land where, two thousand years ago, his Master walked. Many times, Cardinal Tagle would be deeply and visibly moved as we traced the life of Christ through Jerusalem's historical sites. In turn, as these pages will bear out, he would give very moving reflections and sermons. As he was wont to do, as observers point out, he was speaking from his heart. Perhaps like his Lord.

The second reason is the theme that the Cardinal chose for the pilgrimage. There were three groups that journeyed with him that year. Logistically, handling these groups, which totaled to about 90 persons, was almost humanly impossible. Miraculously, however, in the land where once upon a time miracles were a regular spectacle, the group coalesced harmoniously around their shepherd. Many of them had already gone to Jerusalem before. But not around this theme. The usual pilgrimage highlighted the

Via Crucis or the Way of the Cross, which is the Lord's passion and death. The cardinal, however, wanted to take the theme of *Via Lucis* or the Way of Light. This would include Pope John Paul II's Mysteries of Light. But what the cardinal meant by his chosen theme was to approach the life of our Lord from the perspective of the resurrection. That is, a life suffused with light, hope, and joy. We are Easter people, he would always remind the faithful. We follow the Lord filled with the hope of the Easter morning.

And so we trekked, trod, and trudged through the Holy City, following the cardinal and his way of light. We felt blessed and graced. We only wished there were more of us to benefit from the deep and hope-filled reflections of the cardinal on our lives and struggles as followers of Christ. Through this book that wish is finally fulfilled.

—Fr. Emmanuel Alfonso, SJ
Executive Director
Jesuit Communications, Philippines

Editor's Note

Texts in sans-serif font originally appeared in Tagalog, the native language of the Philippines. They are translated here but appear in a different font to indicate a change of voice.

Introduction

Our guides have reminded us many times about the disposition that we need to have as spiritual pilgrims. Here in the Holy Land, while we cannot totally discount the touristic aspect of this pilgrimage, it is still good to be reminded that the spiritual and human renewal that is at the core of every pilgrimage should not be forgotten.

As we said in the orientation in Manila a few days ago, a pilgrimage to the Holy Sites, especially those associated with Jesus and the great men and women of our Judeo-Christian faith, is first of all an assurance to us that our faith is historically based. Our faith is not a product of human imagination and invention alone. The pilgrimage should affirm our faith, edify it, assure us that it is real, that it makes a difference in history. That's the first point to consider.

The second is, as we engage in the geographic tour, we should be mindful of our interior pilgrimage, the pilgrimage into our hearts. As we go to the holy places, let us be reminded of the events in our lives that may be very similar to the events in the lives of the Jewish people, the early Christians, Jesus, Mary, or Joseph. Their experiences are repeated in our lives. Knowing how they were able to respond in faith to the demands not only of God but also of the culture and the situations they had to face, we may be inspired to grapple with our questions, our concerns, our needs, our family situations, as we join Jesus and these holy men and women.

Finally, let this pilgrimage also be a journey toward communion with each other and communion with many other people, those who are here in the Holy Land right now and those who are not with us. Let us bring the prayers, the concerns and needs, the hopes and joys, and the sorrows of our family members, our friends, our loved ones. We remember the sick, the abandoned, those who are struggling with meaning in life. Let us unite ourselves with our brothers and sisters who are still recovering from the effects of typhoons Pedring and Quiel, especially in Bulacan, Pampanga, and Nueva Ecija. We unite ourselves with our brothers and sisters in Eastern Turkey who have just experienced an earthquake that resulted in a great loss of lives; a good number of people are dead, missing, or injured. We also join our brothers and sisters in Thailand; Bangkok is now flooded. So we bring with us a heart that is big enough, like the heart of Christ, to have space, to find space for brothers and sisters who are in need of the grace of light, peace, and meaning.

With these reminders, we hope we can make this journey joyful yet prayerful. Let it be a moment to learn but also a moment to be led into an internal journey of faith and love.

Pilgrimage Schedule

Day ONE	Nazareth
Day TWO	Mount Tabor
Day THREE	Cana
Day FOUR	Jordan
Day FIVE	Jericho
Day SIX	Jerusalem
Day SEVEN	Emmaus

Mary said, "Behold, I am the handmaid of the Lord. May it be done to me according to your word." Then the angel departed from her.

—Luke 1:38

Day One

ANNUNCIATION

The account of the annunciation that we hear over and over again from St. Luke has now become concrete to us. We are here now, where it happened, in that place called Nazareth. This place invites us to deep silence. How we wish we could spend hours here with our eyes closed, with our minds filled with the Spirit, imagining that day when this humble lady, Mary, was visited by the angel.

According to St. Paul, at the designated time called "the fullness of time," God sent His Son, born of a woman by the power of the Holy Spirit. The designated time. The fullness of time. What makes time full? Time becomes full when there is an eruption of love. Time is perfectly completed when the hour brims with the fullness of love. It happened here in this quiet place, the fullness of history when the fullness of God's love was manifested in the descending of His Son. The Word would be spoken as flesh. There is nothing more to say. God would give all, God would say all, all

* Homily at the Basilica of the Annunciation, Nazareth.

of his love would be spoken. It was spoken here. There is nothing left for God. He gave His begotten Son and time was fulfilled.

But here also we see the fullness of love in Mary, in her capacity to receive God's full love, and in full love also to say, "I am the handmaid of the Lord." The love of God was met by the full love of Mary in this exchange of love that made the Word truly flesh. In the power of the Spirit, eternity and history have met right here. We are in a sacred place because it is filled with love, divine love, human love. Let us therefore recall our deep experiences of love, our annunciations that made us tremble like Mary, that also made us capable of loving here. I ask the married people: Ladies, when you were being wooed, that was like an annunciation: Were you tickled pink? And you guys, when your loved one accepted your proposal, that was also annunciation. It is just the same with us priests, I don't know why, but you felt you are being called. Those are moments of annunciation, God's love coming to us, enabling us to respond in love.

We bring to our prayer those people who are questioning God's love; those who consider God distant, not coming to them, not sending angels as bearers of Good News, and those whose hearts are hardened. May they learn the ways of Mary, how to open their hearts to the mystery of love. And may they discover that in our respective fullness of time, God meets us in love. May we all meet God in love.

Prayer: **St. Joseph**

Let us entrust one another to the loving care of St. Joseph the Worker. We pray in a special way for priests and seminarians. The house of Joseph in Nazareth was considered the first seminary, where Jesus was formed

* Exhortation at St. Joseph's Church, Nazareth.

in obedience to God, in working for the kingdom of God. And from that home, he was sent on mission.

Saint Joseph is also the person to whom we should pray if we want a happy death. With his help, we pray for those who are preparing to face death—the terminally ill, those who are in precarious situations. And we pray for ourselves for truly every day we are a step closer to death. May we find death as the fulfillment of life, life in God, life in God's presence. Amen.

TRANSFIGURATION

In the tradition of the Jewish people, the mountain is not just a geographic spot. It is not merely about the place. It is associated with the presence of the divine. That's why mountains are privileged places for prayer, for an encounter with God. In biblical times, God usually revealed his love, his identity, on a mountain.

The transfiguration of Jesus, according to tradition, happened on this mountain, Mount Tabor, and this episode in the life of Christ is quite significant not only for Christ but also for the disciples, for us who follow in the steps of Jesus Christ. Jesus had just openly talked to the disciples about his coming passion and death. He talked about a dark moment they should prepare for. He would be handed over to the chief priest, the leaders of the temple. He would be accused and he would be put to death.

* Talk at the Church of the Transfiguration, Mount Tabor.

Put yourselves in the place of the disciples. Say you are Peter, Andrew, John, or James, and you left everything to follow Jesus. You left father, boats, nets, your whole life to follow Jesus. Then one day he tells you that the one you are following will be condemned as a criminal. How would you feel? A part of you will say, "*God forbid! No! This is not true. Tell us that you are joking. Tell us that this is just a product of your nightmare. Maybe you need to talk it over with a psychiatrist. Maybe you just lost some calories. Wake up, Jesus*!" But it instilled fear and a bit of disappointment in the disciples.

After that moment of disclosure, with Jesus telling his close friends the truth about himself, which caused fear and doubt among them, he brought his three closest friends—Peter, James, and John—to this mountain. Now we are not only three but almost a hundred, and Jesus brought us here. We are his friends. On this mountain, he was transfigured before his friends' very eyes. It was a moment of revelation.

According to the Gospel of St. Luke, Jesus' appearance changed, and his clothing became dazzling white, light, glory, *Via Lucis,* the way of the light. We have just taken the path to light, but remember the one who appears glorious is the one who will one day be arrested, humiliated, and killed. But who is this person? Who is this Jesus that his friends followed? Is he a maverick? Is he adventurous? Is he one of those who want to make a living out of preaching? Is he a crazy spiritual guru who wants to have a following and to have his name and fame spread by his friends? Who is this? I'm sure the disciples entertained these questions. Who is this man that we are following? At one moment he talks about death, another moment he becomes glorious. Who is he? And he talks with Moses and Elijah—Moses, the giver of the law, and Elijah the great prophet. The law and the prophets, the summary of the Scriptures. What we call the Old Testament is personified in these two. Now they are talking to Jesus. What are they talking about?

That's the reason we chose St. Luke. Of all the gospels, it is only St. Luke who tells us what the three were talking about. They were talking about the exodus of Jesus, what he was going to accomplish in Jerusalem.

Jesus was right, after all. He was not fooling his disciples when he said that he would be arrested and killed in Jerusalem. Moses and Elijah were talking about the same thing. They were talking about the dark night of death. Look at this mystery. They were talking about the dark night of death as Jesus was bathed in glorious light, and this happened when Jesus was praying, when he was in deep communion with God. When you are in prayer, your countenance changes. When you are in deep communion with God, your face, your person exudes light. That was the experience of the apostles with Jesus in deep prayer, after realizing that he was going to face his death.

And then from the cloud came a voice. Who is this Jesus? "This is my beloved Son." Now you know who he is, the one who will die is my beloved Son, the one who will go through his exodus in Jerusalem is my Son. And the voice said, "Listen to Him." He's telling you the truth and the body that you see bathed in light is the same body that will be crucified.

This mountain is special to God. Here, the Father speaks to the disciples who are worried about continuing the path of discipleship. Here, the Father reveals who Jesus truly is. Here, we are given hope that every crucifixion, if borne in obedience to the Father and for love of neighbor, is really life-giving, glorious. The crucifixion will still happen; the transfiguration did not erase the death of Christ. But now we know the one who will die is not a criminal. He is truly the Son of God and we have to listen to him because after this he will say, "If you want to be my disciple, you have to deny yourself, take up your cross, and come follow me." You cannot stay on Mount Tabor, you have to follow me. You have to follow me on my exodus to Jerusalem, and there, beholding my body hanging on the cross, you will remember Mount Tabor and say, "This is the glorious body of the Son of God."

Maybe on this mountain of the Transfiguration we can in a way recap the experience of the day. We started in Nazareth, the place of Mary and Joseph and the place where Jesus grew up. That's why he was known as the Nazorean. Who are Batangueños here? Do we have anybody of Ilocano roots? Any Bicolano, Manileño, Ilonggo, Caviteño, Pangasinense? As you can see, even now our identity is usually linked to the place of our origin. It is the same with Jesus. He comes from Nazareth. He grew up in Nazareth. He is to be known as the Nazorean. It looks mysteriously simple from our perspective, but at the time it could've caused a lot of darkness to Mary and Joseph.

The coming of light brings darkness. We have just been to Nain, where Jesus brought the light of life to a widow who had lost her son. We looked at the place. How dark it was with the church closed and not a single Christian seeming to be in charge. Now we come to the Mount of Transfiguration, the glory that will come when the Son of God faces his cross.

Let us not be depressed. The reality is that when the light comes from above, when the light comes from God, we human beings cannot see it as light. Our norms for what is bright do not always correspond with the light of God. That's why even in Christian tradition the great men and women of prayer, the masters of prayer and spirituality, went through the dark night of the senses, the dark night of the soul. But it is darkness that washes human beings. It is dark to us because the light comes not from us but from God. If we can still see the light, it might not be divine. If it is truly from God, then it strikes us as darkness, and Mary is one of our best guides. So many things remained, humanly, to Mary.

Many times in the Gospel of St. Luke we are told that she did not understand, but "she kept all these things in her heart." She pondered, humanly speaking, darkness but with the eyes of faith. It is light that human eyes cannot see. Here, Peter did not know what he was talking about. How can you, humanly speaking, make sense of a heavenly apparition, a heavenly revelation? But you can see how the divine enters as light in ordinary villages like Nazareth, in an ordinary workroom like that of Joseph, and on an ordinary mountain like Tabor.

My dear brothers and sisters, at the end of this day let us reflect. As we go back to our respective homes, as you continue to rest and pray, try to reflect on your own "Nazareths," on your own Nains; try to go back to your own Mount Tabor, where God came as pure gift and pure light but we did not recognize the light and so we trembled before what appeared to be darkness.

In fact, many of us have probably experienced that when light came we said, "Depart from me!" We couldn't stand the light. But without that light, how dark our darkness will be. So let us continue pondering like Mary, Peter, James, John, Joseph. In our dark experiences, let there be light. See the light, the Lord might be there, the beloved Son, listen to him, open your ears. In the darkness, light comes in the mysterious love of the Father.

Let me close with a personal sharing. Ten years ago, when I was told that I was being named bishop of Imus, I did not see the appointment as light. I saw it only as darkness, and I cried and cried. Then I said, "No!" I thought it would be foolish and reckless of me to say "yes." I was called again and offered the post again. It remained dark because I was looking at myself, my capacities, my weaknesses, my sinfulness. I knew myself. But I was greatly consoled by the nuncio, who, by the way, is now the apostolic delegate here in Jerusalem. He embraced me and said, "I know this will be difficult for you. I know this will not make your life easier, but believe." Believe! That was the only thing he asked of me. Just believe. And with all the energies left in me, I tried to believe.

After ten years, it happened again! By now, though, they have learned how to deal with me. When I was called to the office, I asked the secretary, "How much time are you giving me to think about it?" He said, "No, you have already been appointed. We're informing you, and you accept." How come when light comes, darkness sets in?

But perhaps darkness is necessary so that the purity of the gift, the light that has not come from us, is preserved. If the light comes and it is met by my own light, then I would not know whether the light is of my own making or is a gift. This is a simple experience of mine. Maybe you have more dramatic experiences of light coming and you feel you are in the dark when it is truly light.

> Then from the cloud came a voice that said, "This is my chosen Son; listen to him!" After the voice had spoken, Jesus was found alone. They fell silent and did not at that time tell anyone what they had seen.
> —Luke 9:35-36

Prayer: Mysteries of Joy

The first joyful mystery is the Annunciation of the Angel Gabriel to Mary.

The angel was a messenger of God, the messenger of good news, news-bearing light. What is that news? It is that the Savior of the world will be sent from the

* Rosary prayed on the way to the Mount of Beatitudes.

Father, the fullness of time has come. But who can see angels, who can hear angels, and who can accept the messages of angels? Only a person like Mary, a virgin who is totally open and available. We can be the recipients of light if we are as open and as available to do the will of God as Mary was.

The second joyful mystery is the Visitation.

We have two women meeting each other, Mary running to Elizabeth in an act of compassion. Both of them are with child. Through the work of God, these two women who had no opportunities, as human beings, to bear children at their particular moments in life, are now with child. Filled with the Spirit-bearing life, they are prophets and they meet in order to sing praises to God. The Magnificat of Mary is a prophecy of how God takes care of His people, especially of the lowly. It is a prophetic warning to those who do not plan, think, and decide in harmony with God. Are we bearers of God? Are we filled with the Spirit when we encounter people? How do we conduct the many visitations that the Lord wants us to engage in in our daily life?

The third joyful mystery is the birth of our Lord Jesus.

The Word became flesh and dwelt among us. When God spoke His Word in the fullness of time, that Word assumed the form of a human being. God enters human history and assumes the human condition. There is nothing human, except sin, that God did not enter. What a wonderful thing for humanity to realize that everything in us has been touched by the presence of God and everything in us has entered the very life of God. We are saved by such love. Who are we to deserve this love that has the Creator, now present among us as a creature, humbly loving us to life?

The fourth joyful mystery is the Presentation of the Child Jesus in the Temple.

In obedience to the law, Mary and Joseph brought their firstborn son to be presented to God in the temple. Again we behold the humility of the Word-made-flesh; the lawgiver now is a human being, and so is subject to the law and obeys the law. The parents offered to God two pigeons, the offering of a poor family. But the presentation is all about Jesus being revealed as the light to the nations. This boy, innocent and haunted down by a crazy Herod, is truly the light of the nations. Simeon saw in him the fulfillment of the prophecy. When we look at the children of the poor, what do we see? Do we see problems? Do we see trouble? Do we see those who pose a lot of difficulties to society? Or do we see the bearers of light in humble persons like the baby Jesus?

The fifth joyful mystery is the Finding of the Child Jesus in the Temple.

What did Mary and Joseph find in the temple? It was not just their son Jesus, a boy of twelve years. They found someone, a mystery, someone who at a tender age had a clear vision that he belonged to someone who may be called "Abba" and that his life was supposed to be spent on the concerns of Abba. They found not only their child but a true Son, the true Son of the Father. If people find us, what will they see in us? And if we do search for people, do we search for them as children of God, especially the lost, the confused? How do we treat them? Do we find in them children of the Father in search of their mission in life? Mary and Joseph, look for us, and when you see us, may you find us true to our mission.

Day Two

THE FIRST MIRACLE

According to the Gospel of St. John this beautiful and sacred place called Cana was the site of the first miracle or sign that Jesus performed. Significantly, Jesus' first sign was set in the context of a marriage celebration.

This first miracle performed by Jesus in his ministry in this Galilean territory is filled with meaning. In fact, even if we go through different biblical commentaries on this event, we find different interpretations. All of them are right because no single interpretation can capture the depth of this event. And we are here, not only the married people who will renew their commitment to one another later, but even those who are not married. We're all part of this event. We're all part of this explosion of God's light and grace in the first sign that Jesus performed, inviting people to faith.

For me, it's significant that Jesus' first miracle happened in the context of a wedding. In the world of the Jews, the wedding was

* Homily at the Church of the First Miracle, Cana

not only a social or cultural event, not just the coming together of a man and a woman and of two families. In the biblical tradition, the wedding is a symbol of God's covenant with His people. Even in the Old Testament, many images are used by the prophets to talk about God's fidelity and covenant love with His people. One of their favorite images is of a wedding because covenant love, the commitment unto death between husband and wife, captures very well how much God loves us.

This covenant relationship in the Old Testament is captured by the simple formula, "I will be your God, and you will be my people." With that promise of God, Israel becomes His very own and they now share the same destiny. In Filipino we have that beautiful song, "I am yours, you are mine." With that covenant relationship, the friends of God became the friends of Israel, the enemies of Israel also became the enemies of God. They shared life and became one.

Jesus inaugurates his ministry in the context of a wedding in order to impress upon us that he comes to bring a new covenant with the new people. The covenant that was ignored because of sinfulness is now being restored. There is a new offer that will culminate in Jerusalem: "This is the covenant in my blood, this is my body for you, this is my blood for you." The Eucharist is covenantal. It is nuptial, too, and we, receiving his body and blood, will become his body, the nuptial relationship between Jesus and his people.

This, in a way, imposes a heavy responsibility on married people. Your relationship is not meant simply to provide stability to society, as we always say. As Christians, we have the prompting mission to remind everyone of how much God loves His people. It is not just for your smooth human relationship that you will do this, but this is your path to holiness. This is your way of proclaiming to the world how much God loves us.

In the covenant relationship between a man and woman, hopefully people will be reminded of God's covenant with us.

It is not just the priest, the religious, who are called to holiness. All of us, especially married people, are too. Just living with each other demands holiness. You cannot survive a day of committed love if you do not rely on God's grace and if you do not open yourself to Jesus' way of loving. So you are holy and you are precisely called to holiness in marriage. You are to mirror God's love. I hope you will impart this to your children who will get married in the future. Marriage is not merely a social and cultural convention; it is a spiritual, covenantal mission.

That is why, at your renewal vow, you'd say, "You are mine and I am yours. Your joy is my joy, your suffering is my suffering, your dreams are my dreams, your hopes are my hopes. But as for your outstanding debts, pay them yourself!"

Come to think of it, that was how Jesus loved us. He assumed the debt that we had to pay and suffered the pains that we should have borne. That's marriage, that's covenant. Even your debt is my debt, your death is my death. But, as in many marriages, the wine could run out. In some marriages the wine ran out after the first day. You realize how much or how little water I have in my jar.

And that's okay. We don't need to pretend that the jars are always filled to the brim. If you say that, nobody will believe you, so there is no need to hide it from God and from each other. But the beautiful thing is that Jesus can fill the jars with water and transform the water into wine, which is a symbol of celebration. The emptiness and the dryness of the jars are now turned into joy because of the power of the Word of Jesus.

We have to remember today not only ourselves but also our many relatives and friends, whether in marriage or outside of it. I bring to our celebration priests and religious who are also called to covenant love in our mission. Our jars can also become empty.

We lack patience, we need patience. We need kindness. We need long suffering; some even need money to buy food, and the purses are empty. They need bread to feed their children, but the covered sides are empty. They have dreams of sending their children to school, but the opportunities are not there. Oh, there are so many empty jars, but Mary sees them. Just like an attentive mother, she will not miss seeing an empty jar. She approaches Jesus, and his response is enigmatic: "Woman, what is this to you and to me?" In plain language, "Woman, what business is this to you and so what if they are out of wine?" This is not a rude statement at all, for the meaning comes next when he says, "My time has not yet come." Jesus operates within the time of God.

Yesterday we talked about the fullness of time, the hour of God. Jesus was very much aware of that. His mission was in the hands of God. Whenever the Father sees it is your time, then it is your time. And Mary, the ever-gracious woman, saw the lesson and told the people, "Do whatever he tells you." Those are the last words of Mary as recorded in the Bible.

"Do whatever he tells you." Those words echo until now. If you do what he tells you to do, miracles will happen. But you have to be there to do what he tells you. If he tells you to carry six gallons of water, do so, and miracles will happen. If he says so, do it, and the water will turn into wine.

Now Jesus comes to renew us so we can become the new people of the new covenant. And you, married people, will be a living reminder of what Jesus did. May you be the miracle that the world is waiting for. In many parts of the world, marriage is being thrown out the window. They say it is not only an empty jar, it is a useless jar. But if they see loving and joyful people living their faith in their married commitment, then the world will know there will always be wine, there's always reason to celebrate.

On a personal note, I have been really blessed. I officiated at the twenty-fifth wedding anniversary of my parents. I had been ordained at the time. The celebration was a very simple affair. We did not plan anything, but our bishop then, Bishop Felix Perez, insisted. He said, "Twenty-five years? You should do something!" So we celebrated Mass in the small chapel of the Bishop's House in Imus, with maybe only ten guests, mostly relatives. I felt privileged to have officiated at the renewal of my parents' love for each other. Then as a bishop, I officiated at their golden wedding anniversary, and last August, they celebrated their fifty-fifth.

If you think it's special only for you, it is extra-special for the children! I cannot put into words the experience of asking my father, "Do you renew your commitment to my mother?" and then of asking my mother, "Are you willing to renew your commitment to this man, my father?" But there I was, confused in a way. You don't know who you are. Are you the son or are you the priest? But somehow you know the miracle is real. Whether here in Cana or anywhere else we find ourselves, where there is love and where there is patience to fill jars with water, Mary is there, reminding us to "do whatever he tells you." And please share your wine, first with your family and then with the many people who are thirsting for the wine of the covenant in Jesus.

Let us pause before we do the renewal of vows. Let us be grateful to God and let us prepare our hearts to embrace this holy mission.

Prayer: **False Gods**

Carmel is associated with the great prophet Elijah. There are many things that we can learn from Elijah in the Bible but one thing that is of lasting legacy for us is that Elijah showed people who the true God is and he presented himself as the mouthpiece and messenger of the one and only God. In the face of the prophets of other gods, especially Baal, and in the

* Points given at Elijah's Cave, Stella Maris Church, Mount Carmel.

encounter with the prophets, you see how God won; God showed Himself as the only true God.

The problem that Elijah encountered continues in our time. There are many false gods being presented to us, and the sad thing is, they also have their prophets whose voices are sometimes louder and bolder, and so they are able to win people over to their side.

For example, some people now would rather worship in the new "cathedrals": parks, spas, malls. They spend so much time there but find that fifteen minutes spent in a church to worship God a waste of time. They can watch soap operas for three hours but they fall asleep after the second or third Hail Mary in a decade of the rosary.

The battle fought by Elijah continues. The false gods look attractive to the world, but we need more Elijahs who will defend the true God and ensure the joy and commitment to the true God.

We are here on this mountain. If there's something we can ask from God through Elijah, it is for a share of the spirit of Elijah so that we can boldly proclaim who God is. Let us not be afraid, in the face of all adversaries, to proclaim who God is, the only true God, the one we have discovered in Jesus. Let our Blessed Mother guide us in the defense of the faith and in proclaiming the true God.

We are not here for just a visit. As we leave this cave, may we possess the spirit of Elijah, and wherever we are, may we not be ashamed of God and may we offer to God the praise, the thanksgiving, and the sacrifice that God deserves. Please, do not trade the true God. People who exchange the true God for false gods eventually regret it. There's only one God and we should be faithful to Him.

Let us now pause and commit ourselves to God. For our prayers, our response is:

"Make us Your prophets, Lord."

This is indeed the will of My Father that all who see the Son and believe in Him may have eternal life and I will raise them up on the last day. Lord Jesus, faith in You is the salvation of the world. Help us to believe and proclaim what we believe. Let us pray to the Lord—

Make us Your prophets, Lord.

They devoted themselves to the apostles' teaching and fellowship, to the breaking of bread and prayers. Make us loyal to the faith and tradition we have received from the apostles. Let us pray to the Lord—

Make us Your prophets, Lord.

Always be ready to make your defense to anyone who demands from you an accounting for the hope that is in you. Help us to keep the faith pure and uncompromised. Let us pray to the Lord—

Make us Your prophets, Lord.

"If I, then, your Lord and teacher, have washed your feet, you also ought to wash one another's feet for I have given you an example that you also should do as I have done to you." Grant that our faith may lead us to an active concern for the welfare of our brothers and sisters. Let us pray to the Lord—

Make us Your prophets, Lord.

Lord Jesus, Word of the Eternal Father, Word of Life, You became man to offer Yourself as the Way to Salvation. Give us the courage to study our Faith, live it in justice and charity, and defend it from error, You who live and reign forever and ever. Amen.

Our Father. . . .

Let us commend ourselves to our Blessed Mother, the bearer of Jesus who is the Truth. May she guide us in proclaiming the truth about God and about Jesus.

Hail Mary. . . .

And as one community, let us profess our faith in the true God and may we have the spirit of Elijah in proclaiming this same faith with courage, firmness, and joy.

Apostles' Creed. . . .

Glory Be. . . .

In the name of the Father and of the Son and of the Holy Spirit. Amen.

PLACE OF FIRST ENCOUNTERS, FIRST LOVE

Aside from introducing us to the place, our guide emphasized that what we are doing is really living the Bible, experiencing it, and being able to say "I was there" so that whenever we read these episodes we can say, the episode is in me now; it is not of the past. These are not episodes that are in the past and gone, but refreshed merely by memories. These events are happening at this very moment.

* Talk on boat ride at the Sea of Galilee.

The Sea of Galilee figured prominently in the life and ministry of Jesus Christ. In fact, it was somewhere here that he first encountered Peter and his brother, Andrew, and their business partners, John and James. It was somewhere here that Jesus called his first disciples. We are very close to the place of first encounters, first love. This morning at Cana we renewed the marriage commitment of the couples. Remember your Galilees.

Do you remember when you first met? That was your Galilee. Do you remember the feeling of intensity when your eyes first met, and he said, "Do you care for halo-halo?"* And you, even if you were feeling chilly, replied, "Of course, as long as there is ice cream on it." That's your Galilee. Each one of us has a Galilee. That special moment of falling in love, that special moment when we were captured by someone, someone different from ourselves.

In the case of Peter, Andrew, James, and John, they met someone greater than they were, someone so great they were able to leave behind family, business, a terrain that was familiar to them, and nothing was the same again, for they became fishers of human beings.

After a tortuous relationship with his apostles, highlighted by denials and betrayals, Jesus said to Mary of Magdala at the tomb of the resurrection: tell Peter and my disciples that I will see them in Galilee. Indeed, the risen Lord appeared to them as though saying, "You have faltered, but let us start again, let us begin again."

I am sure that you have gone through a number of storms in your married lives, the memory lapses, such as, "Is that your wife/husband?" and "Oh no, I don't recognize him/her!" Where one once had the Coca-Cola bottle body figure, it has now become a Coke in a can. That is why you cannot distinguish

* Halo-halo is a Filipino dessert with multiple ingredient combinations. Ice cream is but one optional topping.

it. You are just like Peter: "No, I don't know him." But we are in Galilee, so let us start all over again. This is the place of first encounters, first loves, and loves renewed, encounters leading to deeper love, deeper commitment. I hope this is true not only of married people but even of those who are not married, those who are just starting, and those with a different commitment in life.

It is special to be here. I can hear Jesus saying, "Come, follow me." In this place that voice will never be erased. Anyone who visits here must hear it. We must hear, "Come, follow me."

But we know that following Jesus, especially if the calling started here at the Sea of Galilee, will involve a lot of storms, as our Gospel reading proclaimed. There was a storm. Jesus was sleeping, and imagine, those who were supposed to know this place very well, the fishermen, panicked. For someone who was supposed to be familiar with this situation, knowing the course of the wind, spending much of their time in the sea where their livelihood depended, they were the ones who were very scared. As if it was not their source of life anymore. They were afraid that it could be their tomb and so they cried out to the Lord. They did not merely wake him up and ask help from him. They reproved him. "Are you not bothered? You are just sleeping there. What kind of master are you?"

Wives, what would you do if your husbands just slept all through it? Surely, you'd throw him into the sea. Husbands, when you come home and dinner is not ready because your spouses have been sleeping all day, what would you do? If you would go to a parish where the priest just sleeps all day—morning, noon, nighttime—what would you do to the priest? You would get frustrated, especially if you have risked something to be there. And look at what happened: Peter and the disciples were the picture of a group filled with fear.

When you are fearful, your focus is on yourself. Fear draws attention away from other people and to the self. Fear leads to self-preservation, and faith is diminished. Because faith is abandonment of myself to the other, and fear is I will not abandon myself, especially to a lord and master who is sleeping.

There's another episode that happened here at the Sea of Galilee. Again there was a storm. It was after the multiplication of the loaves and fishes. Jesus told the disciples to get on the boat ahead of him while he stayed on the ground to pray. In the middle of the night there was a storm, and Jesus, seeing the disciples from a distance, walked toward them. When they saw him coming near, they thought he was a ghost and they became afraid again—afraid of the storm and afraid of this alien creature. When you are afraid, the last guest you would want to come is a ghost. As if being scared is not enough, you are also being spooked by a ghost. But this is the way of the Lord, the Lord who sleeps or the Lord who comes in the form of a ghost.

According to Bible scholars, the boat is an image of the church. So very early in the life of the church the early Christians experienced many storms, persecutions, defections, heresies. Maybe there were times when they felt Jesus did not care, that he was distant, or that he was just enjoying his sleep, his slumber in the presence of God in heaven, unmindful of what his followers were experiencing. Don't we all experience that? Married couples, your mission in life is to take care of your kids, and sometimes, even your spouse. And, perhaps, no matter how long you've been married together, if you think you can relax after forty or forty-five years, you are mistaken. Storms related to your children or your grandchildren come. The calm waters of the Sea of Galilee seem so hard to find, come so infrequently. And then you pray. You pray hard but the answer you're waiting for does not always come. What comes to us is a ghost, or we begin to feel that the Lord is asleep and then we panic, *"Lord, we are afraid, we feel alone."*

While we are at this lake, let us recall those moments in our lives. But let the challenge of Jesus be heard again. Let the words that Jesus spoke here ring loud and clear: *"O you of little faith. What is the use of fear? Will fear save you?"* What is needed is faith, instead of thinking of yourself, instead of engaging in self-pity, instead of planning self-preservation. Faith. *"I am near, I am coming to you. Believe that I am seeing your boat being tossed. Believe that I am here even when I am sleeping. The important thing is, I am with you."* The prophecy is Emmanuel, God is with us.

My Scripture teacher told us that when Jesus said, *"Why were you afraid? Why don't you believe,"* he did not mean at the time *"I am here, so the storm will pass." No.* The point of Jesus is "I am here. I am here with you even if the boat sinks. I will never leave you. You would not go down alone. I am with you."

Faith doesn't mean that all problems will be solved. Faith doesn't mean that all our prayers will be answered according to our wishes. Faith means *"I am already at peace because I am not alone; God is with me."*

We may not have to sink, but if we do, Jesus is with us. It is better to have sunk, rather than be afloat without him. Sometimes, we want to keep afloat without him.

This is hard teaching. As I'm uttering these words I am trembling from within because I know I am not capable of this faith. I want the seas of my life to be smooth, just like all of you. I want the winds to be a mild breeze, not too strong to make me shiver or to topple me down. I want sunsets that soothe the eyes but not total darkness. If we can only freeze time and moments and stay in places where there is comfort, we would do that. But life and mission are not like that, I guess, for a purpose, so that we may know what faith means. And remember we can trust in Jesus; he was true to his promise.

In truth, we should feel sorry for him. When he was in the storms of his life, he was alone. Yet, in the storms of our lives, he was walking beside us. When the storms got into his life, people turned away from him. And here is Peter who said to

Jesus, "and you just kept on sleeping," and when Jesus was about to die, he was asleep. And Jesus said, "So you could not keep watch with me for one hour?" Later Peter will say, "I do not know the man. I do not recognize him." That is why it is good to revisit Galilee—for us to recover pure faith and first loves and encounters.

Let us enjoy this place, filled with human realities, with the presence of Jesus. The next time you experience storms in your life, remember this boat ride and remember how Jesus comes. You don't need to ask him to come. He will come because he sees and he is faithful. He is Emmanuel, God with us. Let us pause and look around and offer to God our feeble, fragile faith, trusting in His words that if you have faith even as small as a mustard seed, you can tell this mountain to move and it will move. Faith.

Day Three

THREE BAPTISMS

Before renewing our baptismal vows, we want to be reminded of at least three types of baptism.

The first is the baptism that Jesus underwent here with John the Baptist as the so-called minister. That first baptism by water was quite a scandal because the baptism of John the Baptist was for the forgiveness of sins. Those who came to John the Baptist were the known sinners. The tax collectors, those who cheated people, came here to be washed clean, and Jesus joined them. That was a scandal because he claimed to be the Son of God. He claimed to be the one sent by the Father. So, why did he beg John the Baptist for baptism? To which John the Baptist said, "No!" You should be the one to baptize me, and not me baptizing you. But Jesus insisted, "Let it be, in order to fulfill all righteousness."

Here Jesus showed how he was united to all of us sinners. He was not being baptized by John as an individual. Already at his

* Talk at the River Jordan before the "baptisms" of pilgrims.

baptism, he embraced all of us. He did not deem it below his dignity to be identified with sinners.

Many times we are ashamed to be identified with some people or with some groups. If we see a group of majongeras, we think, "I don't want to sit with them. People might think I'm also a gambler." Or with a group of drunkards, "I don't want to join them, they might think that I am a drunkard." And maybe among us here, we graduated from different universities and tend to be proud alumni. I am a Lasalista, for instance, having graduated from De La Salle University. And here is an Atenista, from Ateneo de Manila University. But here is one who only graduated from Barangay High School! We should not be thinking that way.

Admittedly, we have the tendency to choose the group with whom we'll be identified. We don't want to be identified with people who are "below" our standards. But Jesus fell in line here, queued up with sinners, already showing us the great love of God. This was the incarnation all over again. So it was not for the forgiveness of his sins; he was already showing how much he loved us and how much he was united with us.

But there's a second baptism of Jesus—the baptism in his blood. He told the disciples, the baptism I am meant to undergo, and that is the baptism on the cross, is no longer with this water but in my own blood that will wash away the sins of the world.

That's a more difficult type of baptism. Again, it is not really for himself. It is for others. Now, to line up with sinners and to be submerged in the water, that's okay. But to be crucified as a criminal with two other criminals, that's something else. And there hangs the word "*INRI.*" That was the name of his crime: "Jesus of Nazareth, King of the Jews." He pretended to be the king of the Jews and for that, for telling the truth, he was crucified. But this baptism, in blood, which brought about a new covenant, this is another thing we commemorate.

Finally, the third baptism is our Christian baptism. Saint Paul, in his letter to the Romans, said: We who were baptized were buried with Christ; we have died with Christ. The old person has died with him, so that we could also rise with him. So, symbolized by the water, our baptism is a form of dying, so that we can emerge into new life.

We therefore thank God for sending Jesus, who, in spite of being the Son of God, embraced our misery to the point of death so that we may live. As we renew our baptismal promises, let us commit ourselves to Jesus, that we will live with him and for him; live his life, imitate him and his compassion and solidarity with people; that we will offer our lives for the good of others. This is what our Christian baptism is all about—new life in God.

Let us now renew our baptismal vows. But before we do the simple rite of renewal, let us pause and prepare our hearts, ourselves—renounce sinfulness and everything that is against the life of Christ, and embrace our faith, living for God, living for the Father, for Jesus, and for the Sprit.

And now let us rise. If this were the Easter Vigil celebration or Easter Sunday Mass, we would have lighted our candles. But, for our purposes here, you can put your right hand on your heart and sincerely say, "I do."

> Do you reject Satan? *I do.*
> And all his works? *I do.*
> And all his empty promises? *I do.*

Let us now turn to our faith.

> Do you believe in God, the Father Almighty, creator of heaven and earth? *I do.*
> Do you believe in Jesus Christ, His only Son, our Lord, who was born of the Virgin Mary, was crucified, died, and

was buried, rose from the dead and is seated at the right hand of the Father? *I do.*
Do you believe in the Holy Spirit, the Holy Catholic Church, the communion of saints, the forgiveness of sins, the resurrection of the body, and life everlasting?
I do.

God, the All-powerful Father of our Lord, Jesus Christ, has given us new birth by water and the Holy Spirit, and has forgiven all our sins. May He also keep us faithful to our Lord, Jesus Christ, now and forever. *Amen.*

> Then Jesus came from Galilee to John at the Jordan, to be baptized by him. John tried to prevent him, saying, "I need to be baptized by you, and yet you are coming to me?" Jesus said to him in reply, "Allow it now; for thus it is fitting for us to fulfill all righteousness." Then he allowed him. After Jesus was baptized, he came up from the water and behold, the heavens were opened [for him], and he saw the Spirit of God descending like a dove [and] coming upon him. And a voice came from the heavens, saying, "This is my beloved Son, with whom I am well pleased."
>
> —Matthew 3:13-17

TRUE BLESSEDNESS

In the Gospel of St. Matthew, the ministry of Jesus begins with the Sermon on the Mount. Tradition says it was in this place that this sermon, this body of teachings, was conveyed by Jesus to the disciples. I don't dare pretend to be Jesus and you the disciples. We are all disciples here and we want to enter the world of the early disciples listening to Jesus. Again the words of Jesus are mysterious. But many people say that in the sermon we find the magna carta of discipleship. If governments and organizations have their magna carta, we also have ours, and this is the path to true discipleship.

The first part begins with the "Beatitudes" or "Macharisms." Both mean being blessed. But what is true blessedness? And what is true happiness? This set of readings is difficult to understand without us entering the world of the disciples. They remembered these teachings of Jesus, but what made them remember was their experience, their search for true blessedness and happiness. Their experience verified the teachings of Christ. These teachings, without the corresponding verification in life, especially in the lives of the disciples, will remain teachings or even abstractions. Of course, coming from Jesus, they are already true, but they acquire a certain weight in the world when those who have heard and acted on them can proclaim them as true.

When I was a student in Washington, DC, I had a spiritual director, Fr. Peter Henriot, a Jesuit priest, who was instrumental in the rediscovery of the social teachings of the church. He told me that at one time in a parish, this was the reading. He proclaimed the gospel and said, "How blessed are the rich? How

* Homily given at Mass offered on Mount of Beatitudes.

blessed are the filthy rich? The reign of God is theirs. Blessed too are those who do not experience any sorrow. Blessed are the proud. Blessed are those who are promiscuous. Blessed are those who take revenge." The people, the congregation, started becoming jittery. They started whispering, "Something is wrong with the gospel, something is wrong." The priest stopped and said, "So, you know! Jesus would not have said those words. You know that is not part of the Good News of Jesus." And then he read the Beatitudes.

He said there was no need for a homily. He sat down and made people experience that. Deep in our hearts, we know where the heart of Jesus lies. But the human and worldly part of us resists this. We are not happy when we are suffering. We are not happy when we are being ridiculed and scorned. We do not want to be always the one to understand and forgive others. We do not want to keep and hold peace when vengeance would have been easier. We do not want to be patient. As said here, "Blessed are the single-hearted." But, as the song goes, "I wish I had two hearts."* We want two, three, four hearts when we only need one. We are also told, blessed are the persecuted for the sake of holiness. Definitely, we do not want to be persecuted.

But how can these Beatitudes be the path to true happiness? The problem is we pay attention only to the first part of the Beatitudes and forget the promise they contain. Why are the poor blessed and happy? Because the kingdom of God is theirs—not the kingdom of this world but a different type of kingdom. Why are the sorrowing happy or blessed? Because they will be consoled by God. They will not be consoled by a beautiful movie or the comforts of shopping or a spa treatment. They will be

* "*Sana dalawa ang puso ko*," a song by Bodjie Dasig has become a pop standard in the Philippines since its original release in 1993. It later became the theme song in a popular movie by the same name.

consoled by God. Why are the lowly happy? Because they will inherit the land, the promised land, the eternal paradise. Why are you blessed when you hunger and thirst for holiness? Because you will have your fill and you will not go hungry anymore. So all this boils down to the last: "Blessed are you when they insult you and persecute you because your reward in heaven is great."

Jesus is teaching us that true happiness is found in belonging to God and allowing God to reign in our life. That's the core of happiness. He is not despising property. He is not telling us to be lazy and not to earn our daily bread. But after we have accomplished all these things, after we have made a name for ourselves, after getting all the adulation, we still will not experience true happiness and blessedness. True happiness is found in Jesus and in belonging to His kingdom. And if Jesus is my joy, if Jesus is my wealth, then even persecution is cause for joy because I am persecuted for his name. The parents among you, when your children get sick, you don't mind losing sleep to watch over them. You're blessed because you share in their suffering. But you'll cry a lot, you're anxious all the time. But that anxiety, that sorrow is joy because you are living in love. When some of us do away with comforts in order to be of help to an ailing parent or a friend, we forgo our plans. But making that sacrifice gives us a different type of joy. The world will tell us, "Oh, you're foolish!" But in our heart we feel blessed and happy. This is the joy that the world cannot give. But it is found by people, who, because they have embraced Jesus, know the meaning of their lives. They know what true blessedness is.

Pope Benedict said, "What did Jesus come to bring us? Did he come to bring us a comfortable life? No!

Did he come to bring us the solutions to all of our problems? No! Did he come to promise a life without any problems, without any trials? No! Jesus came to give us God, God who is love. And those who accept God as love, those who say I need you, God,

I want to belong to You, can bear with anything, with lowliness, with insult, with persecution, because all of these are for God." So while we are here, perhaps we should ask ourselves: What can really make me happy? This is a place to revise our hierarchy of values, our sources of joy and happiness.

Let us concede to the fact that as we get older, we realize that the things we passionately fought for in our youth have lost their values now. Before, we thought that to lose those things would ruin our lives. It does not happen that way at all. That is not the true happiness, and the heart wants to be where the heart of Jesus is. We can simplify the Beatitudes that way—entering the heart of Jesus and letting my heart beat with the heart of Jesus. And when my heart beats with the beating of the heart of Christ, I am happy. I find joy. I am blessed. We ask for that grace.

Once I was asked to give sessions to a group of contemplative sisters. Coming from all over the world, they gathered in the Philippines for a month of renewal. They asked for a week, but I could give only one day of lectures from eight in the morning till five in the afternoon. At the end of the eight hours, I prepared to go back to Cavite. The head of the federation ran after me with an envelope. "No," I said, "I don't need that. You have a lot of expenses during this month. Use it for the sisters." But she was insistent. She said, "Just give this to any needy person who comes to you." "Okay," I said, "for charity, I accept it."

Back in the car, I felt the envelope which was rather thick. A second thought was tempting me and I said to myself, "Too bad, what a waste to give it away. Certainly I worked hard for the sessions. I think I deserve it, at least even a portion of this." The sign of blessedness! It was a good lesson on the Beatitudes. Suddenly the phone rang. It was a former seminarian who was three years ahead of me in the seminary. He said, "Chito, do you remember me?" I said, "Of course!" He said, "I'm now just a simple teacher and my wife has cancer. She'll start her chemotherapy tomorrow. Can you help me?" And I looked at the envelope. "Okay, I will help you." I went to an LBC office to send the money to him immediately; I was even asked for P1,500.00 as "sending fee." I sadly said, "Gosh, I already got nothing of it, and in addition to that, I have to shell out!"

That evening in the seminary, I recounted the story. One of the priests started stroking my back. "Oh, Bishop, you are so dumb!" I thought that I would be praised. How dumb could I be? But that night, I slept with a deep, deep peace. And I realized this is probably the joy, the peace promised by Jesus. You lost your whole day's wages; nothing was left. You even had to shell out. But why are you happy? Why at that point, could you die and say that life was worth it, really? After a few days, that former seminarian was shot while he was teaching in the classroom. He died instantly. I would have regretted it had I not helped him.

So in a way the calling of the Beatitudes is urgent. Don't postpone your belonging to God's rule. When there is a calling to be poor in spirit, to be lowly, to be merciful, to be a peacemaker, grab the opportunity. You will not regret it. You will be happy. You will feel a happiness that the world will call "foolishness." You are so dumb! But in God's own time we will realize it has been His hand at work.

Let us now pause and allow this beautiful place and the teachings of Jesus and the experience of the early disciples to challenge us, to purify us, and to transform us into living witnesses of the joy that belonging to God's kingdom brings us.

"IT IS THE LORD!"

Even if we still have some places to visit tomorrow, we're already giving this mini-recollection as a way of recapping or summarizing this first portion of our pilgrimage, which centers on the Galilean area. In the New Testament, Galilee was the beginning of the ministry of Jesus. From Galilee, he will go to Jerusalem. So tomorrow we go to Jerusalem.

But before we do, please bear in mind our experience of Nazareth, where the angel Gabriel spoke to Mary of the plan of God and her role in it. Remember also the lowly place of Joseph, the place of work that also became the place of the rearing for Jesus, the place of the family that was born out of the fulfillment of God's will, a special type of family. They became a family because they obeyed the will of God. It was not blood but the will of God and their obedience that made them a family.

Then try to recall how this Galilean area became the unfolding of the ministry of Jesus, starting with the Mount of Transfiguration, the moment of the explosion of the light who is Jesus. We visited Cana, another explosion of light, touching again on the family and how it could be the bearer of God's light and the new covenant with the new people. And then Carmel, where the true God was defended by Elijah. We ended yesterday with a boat trip and started reflecting on the significance of the Sea of Galilee.

Now we are here again and we are focusing on some episodes after the death of Jesus Christ. We are standing at the place where the third appearance of the Lord as the risen One, as the triumphant One, as the Holy One from God, happened. Light,

* Points given for the mini-recollection held at the Church of the Primacy of Peter at Tabgha.

the way of the light, happened here—a different type of light, pure light, the dawning of divinity in Jesus Christ, the risen One.

The gospel passage that we chose, which is related to the place, John 21, gives us three points for meditation. The first point concerns the appearance of the risen Lord to the seven disciples. They probably were business partners of Peter. They decided to go fishing. They were expert fishermen but they caught nothing that whole night. Indeed, if we need to learn about fishing, we should turn to Peter. (That is why the type of fish caught here, a kind of tilapia, is called "St. Peter's fish.") For a fisherman—or any worker, for that matter—to invest so much time and effort and not produce anything is really darkness.

But on that early morning, Jesus was standing on the shore to meet this weary group that probably felt they were useless, the night was useless. Jesus was standing there but the apostles did not recognize him. It was therefore not just the darkness of not having caught anything. According to John 20–21, Jesus was there, but the disciples did not realize it was he. Another type of darkness, a blindness. You have someone there, the Son of God, the risen One, and what a pity you do not recognize him.

Just to connect it to our experience, remember the time when Mexican telenovelas were popular in the Philippines? I attended a meeting in Cebu and when I was checking out of the hotel, a famous actor from one of those *telenovelas* came to check in. I think it was Fernando Carillo, who played the irresistible Fernando José on *Rosalinda*. The girls at the counter, they recognized him, left the counter, and ran to him. They fussed over him and even kissed him. I was left alone at the counter without any help, even though I was there first. But they did not recognize me. I asked myself, why is that so? He is Fernando José, with two names. Likewise with me—Luis Antonio. I could be compared with him. He comes from Venezuela, I come from China! But that's the way it is. Not to be recognized. They did not even ask for my autograph. But it's really okay if they don't recognize this thin, Chinese-looking priest. Maybe they thought I was selling insurance and they didn't want to bother with me. But if it is the risen Lord, the One who has changed the course of history, standing there, and they did not recognize him, that would be most unfortunate! The darkness of the night, the weariness of the night, was internalized by the disciples. There was also blindness.

But how did the light come? Jesus asked a simple question that could be irritating: "Children, have you caught anything to eat?" Anyone could see that the boat was empty. If I were Peter, I would have said, "Don't you have eyes? Are you kidding me? Are you teasing me?" And then they said, maybe out of tiredness, "No." A simple No. They had no more energy to argue with Jesus and no more energy to explain a simple No. Nothing. They caught nothing.

And then came something absurd. We know it is Jesus. We know this is the son of the carpenter. We know this is a guru, a rabbi who knows nothing about fishing. From him, however, comes the absurd command, "Cast the net over the right side of the boat and you will find something." And the mystery of it all is, they followed, they did as they were told. Maybe out of desperation, or resignation. "Okay, just be quiet. I will do it. We will do it. Yet the miracle happened and they caught a tremendous number, 153 fish.

That number is significant. 153. In Hebrew they don't use numbers; they use letters. Thus a common practice is to add up the letters in a name or phrase to come up with special numbers. And if you add up the numbers in the phrase "I am God," you get 153! That's why it was not surprising that after seeing the miraculous catch the beloved disciple said to Peter, "It is the Lord." It's not so much the catch, but the presence of someone who directs the catch. It is not about fishing—it is about God's revelation. God reveals himself in the risen Lord to a weary band of poor fishermen. But he reveals himself as the one who is in control, the one who can do marvels even to people who think of themselves as experts. He reveals himself as wisdom to those who think they are wise but can produce nothing with their wisdom. He comes in the form of an absurd director in a business that he has no right to direct. But he comes to us in that humble voice, telling us, "Why don't you try this side?" And the miracle happens.

I'm sure all of us have had not only one night of fruitless labor in our lives, perhaps in our marriages or in our ministries in the church. I will be thirty years a priest in February. In those thirty years certainly there were plenty of nights and days of fruitless labor. Yes, our lives are filled with Peter's experience. We need not worry or despair. Those times are needed.

As I look back at my ministry, those moments when I thought I was not getting the fruits that I anticipated, it was those moments when I could now say the Lord was there as a gentle light. But just like the apostles, often I do not recognize it is the Lord. And because we do not recognize, we do not allow Him to direct our catch. We continue with the status quo. We continue with our habits, comfortable ways of doing things. But he is asking us to cast the net into the other side, to follow his ways, not our ways; His plans, not our plans. And when we obey, God surprises us. "Wow! What a catch!" We realize that in that dark night, there was this glimmer of light, unnoticed but real. It is the Lord.

May I invite you to recall your experiences of fruitlessness. Recall the times when you felt so disheartened and empty. But now open your eyes of faith. Maybe you just did not see God at that time, maybe you just did not hear him say: "Cast your net here."

Before I leave this point, let us learn from the beloved disciple. Peter was the prince of the apostles. Later Jesus would entrust to him the feeding of the sheep. But in this scriptural passage, it was the beloved disciple that taught Peter. Peter did not recognize the Lord. The first one to recognize the Lord was the beloved disciple.

In the Gospel of John, the beloved disciple is not named. In the Christian tradition, we call him "John." But here he is simply called the beloved disciple, the one who was so open to the love of Christ and the one who loved Christ the most. Love enables us to see; love enables us to recognize the God who is love.

That is why I don't believe that love is blind. No. That is negated by our gospel. Who saw Jesus? Not the appointed friends, not the one with authority, but the one with tremendous love.

Once, when I was a seminarian, my classmates and I provided the choral services at a wedding. The bride looked like an angel who had just descended from above. Then we looked at the groom, then at the bride, then back at the groom. What happened here? There seemed to be no match. One classmate suggested, "Let's just accept it. Let's admit it, *love is blind.*" But a wise, elderly classmate said, "Love is blind? Or, maybe we are the ones who are blind!"

That comment generated a whole reflection on our way home. Yes, we were blind because, to us, that guy was a total stranger. We didn't see anything beautiful in him; we didn't recognize a person worthy of love; we didn't see someone precious. But this woman who loves him sees something that we didn't.

On a more serious note, there is a lesson here for us, especially for us bishops and priests. The authority of Peter was not enough. It is not authority that makes us see and recognize the Lord. In the end, it is the love of a disciple that is able to discern the presence of the Lord. When love vanishes, we are blinded, and we won't see the Lord anymore. That's our mission, a mission of light to point the people to the Lord among the weary, the hungry, the poor, the desperate. We should be there to say, "It is the Lord," to bring light to those walking in darkness. But how can we do that? Only when we have love, love for the Lord and love for others; recognition in love—that's how we bring light. That's the first point, and we can spend a whole lifetime reflecting on it.

Let us go to the second point. After that recognition—"It is the Lord!"—Jesus invites them, "Come, have breakfast." Now I want to highlight two important things. First, it is a sign that Jesus is truly risen. He is alive. In the Bible, those who can eat are only those who are alive. If you cannot eat, you are close to death. My parents are both eighty-one. People tell them, "Don't eat this, don't eat that!" Please, if they have an appetite, let them eat. That shows they are alive. I would worry more if they were to lose their appetite. Recall some of the miracles of Christ. Remember that twelve-year-old girl who was brought back to life—what was the first thing he did? He took her to the parents and said, "Give her something to eat." That is a proof, a sign, that the girl is truly alive, if she can eat. So eat. To eat, therefore, is a simple sign that I am truly alive. If I were dead, I would not be eating now. Jesus uses this sign to show that he is truly alive.

Secondly, this is not just a meal. Remember how the disciples abandoned Jesus. They who constituted the first church, the early church, were easily dispersed. They denied Jesus. They protected themselves.

But now Jesus invites them, "Come, have breakfast." Come, let us share food again. Come, let us build our family again. So the risen Lord does not come only to be recognized. One light that the risen Lord gives is the gathering again of a community, of a family, the gathering of a people who have been dispersed for so many different reasons. That is darkness—dispersal, division, discrimination, forgetfulness of each other.

The risen Lord gives us the light of being able to come together again and be centered around the table, the meal. That's why the Eucharist is our table where we are built again and again as a family of God, sharing the same bread, sharing the same cup. The breakfast is no longer fish. It is Jesus himself, his word, his body and blood, to be built up as a community.

What has happened to our family meals? When I was growing up, no meal started without everyone present and the basic unit of the meal was not the plate but the table. You all gathered around the table where you had the bowl of rice, fish, and vegetables that you all shared. Early on you learned how to share. You realized that there were four of you around the table, so you would get only your portion. The miracle was that there were always leftovers. Because there was sharing.

Today, however, many families don't eat together. The basic unit now has become the plate. I have my plate and I go where I want to eat—in front of the TV or the computer, in my bedroom. And the fast-food places are no help. Sometimes at the food court, you will see a family eating together. The father is having Italian food, the mother Chinese, and the child, Japanese. And then we wonder why there is no cohesion. You wonder why there is no more sense of family. I think that one area we must look into is the meal. Father Patrick Peyton used to say, "The family that prays together stays together." I would add, "The family that eats together stays together."

Jesus did that with his apostles. "Come, have breakfast." It was also his way of saying, "Let us break bread; let us share life." Sharing the same food means sharing life and becoming one body, one family. For what sustains me sustains you. What quenches my thirst, quenches your thirst. What fills me fills you. We are one. And if what I eat is poison, what will kill me will kill you. We are one. This is the light that our families need. We have to learn from the wisdom of the ages. We are so preoccupied with things to do, holding our child close to us, holding the McDonald's, but we have lost the fundamentals.

I remember that was the reason I had to be home at seven in the evening. When you were a teenager, especially during summer, you went to many places just for fun and adventure. We even hit Roxas Boulevard, and entered the discotheque with our pairs of shoes tucked in our jackets. But we always punctually went home knowing that family members might be hungry by then. Dinner was not served if one family member was missing. And around the table you don't share only food. The stories of the day are woven into a tapestry called the "family." The table becomes the storage, the reservoir of common memory, of joys and frustrations shared. It becomes food for the family. That's the second point. How can we be the light of Christ in building up families, communities where there is sharing of food, sharing of memories, sharing of dreams, sharing of stories?

The third point is the continuation of the story. After breakfast, after reconstituting the community, now comes commissioning. From recognition to communion, and now to mission. Recognition of the risen Lord, leading to communion around the one table, and now comes mission. Peter was asked by Jesus three times, "Simon, son of John, do you love me more than these?" This is John 21, but in John 13, Jesus tells his disciples that where he is going, they cannot follow him yet. But Peter asks, "Why can't I follow you now?" He is, as it were, already presenting himself even before hearing Christ's call, "Come, follow me."

Once I had to stop an ordination. In the ritual of ordination, the candidate is called first by name. However in this particular ordination, the rector had not even called the candidate yet, but he already stood up and said, "Here I am." I said, "Excuse me, let us stop. Let us go back. It is the calling first." I told the candidate, "You have not been called yet, and you have given your reply already. Wait till you are called."

That's not just a ritual. It is really biblically based, and it happened to Peter. The Lord said, "You cannot follow Me now." And yet Peter presented himself, "Why can't I follow you now? I will lay down my life for you." In the Gospel of John, to lay down one's life for someone means "I am your best friend." It is as if Peter is saying, "Among the twelve here, I am your best friend and the only one willing and ready to lay down my life for you." But Jesus says, "You? You will lay down your life for me? I know you, Peter. I know you. You do not know yourself. You have a caricature of yourself. But I know your heart. I know you will not lay down your life for me. You will deny me." And Jesus was proven right. Jesus knew Peter more than Peter knew himself.

Now, after the resurrection, Jesus asks Peter, "Peter, do you love me more than these?" Do you really love me more than the love of the others? And look at the humility of Peter, born out of, in a way, humiliation. He says, "Yes, Lord, you know that I love you." It's no longer the bold "Yes, I love You!" Instead, "You know my heart, Lord, and there must be a bit of love there for you. I cannot pretend to know myself now. I open my heart to you. You know me." I can hear Psalm 139 here. "Lord you are near, you know my heart. You know where and when I stand, where and when I sit. Lord, you know me and I hope you see the bit of love that I have for you." Now Peter is not just prince of the apostles. Now he is also like the beloved disciple. Jesus wants a profession of love, the power and the authority that come from loving.

So Peter is being transformed into the beloved disciple. It is as though Jesus is telling him, "Peter, I don't need an enumeration, a list, a litany of what you will do for me because I know you. You are not capable. I ask for only one thing. Do you have enough love for me? Do you love me?" And with Peter's profession of love, in reparation for the three moments of denial, love is now reciprocated by Jesus with trust. "Feed my lambs. . . . Tend my sheep." The lambs are the little ones; the sheep, the big ones. Whether small or big, they need to be fed. Feed everyone. Feed especially the sheep because they think they are self-sufficient. They are big in their own estimation. But they need to be fed, just like you, Peter. You used to consider yourself a sheep. But, you see, I needed to feed you. And only after that, with Peter learning the ways of humility, does Jesus again prophesy, "A time will come when somebody will tie your hands and lead you where you'd rather not go." So, you will lose yourself, Peter. When you love, you lose yourself.

The story ends with Jesus saying, "Follow me." Now you can follow me. When you were filled with self, when you were just trying to prove yourself, you had no capacity to follow me. But now you're humbled, you're filled with love, you can follow me. But they remain my sheep, they are not yours. So you will give them the caring that I would want to give you. Feed my sheep, tend my lambs, they are mine. So if you love me, you will love my own. They are my own. If you love me, you will love them too. This is our mission: to feed, to tend in love, for no other reason or motivation, than because we love Jesus.

For this third point, we are brought to the light of mission. But mission becomes light only when it is generated by love, by humility, not by any ambition or desire to prove my worth and my capacities. Only love. So let us look back at our whole lives. First, my experience of recognizing the Lord in our night experiences of weariness and fruitlessness, and then the challenge of the light of communion, family, community, nation building, parish building, church building; and finally, let us reflect on the mission of being the beloved.

I want to end on a personal note. One of the first questions I asked our guide when we reached Tiberius was whether we would go to the place where the miraculous catch after the resurrection happened. "Yes," he said, "we will go to *Mensa Christi*." That gave me a lot of peace because as you know, we bishops have our mottos. We have our coat of arms and then our mottos.

And my motto is, "It is the Lord." And I pray that I will be like the beloved disciple. I'm sure there will be a lot of nights when there will be no catch. But I hope love will keep burning, and when there is love, we recognize the Lord and miracles can happen—in spite of ourselves, in spite of our efforts.

I believe it is that same love that can generate a community, build up a community, and fire up mission. I did not know that when I chose this passage for my motto. I just loved the passage. I did not know that this choice would lead me to a program of life, a program of mission.

And now we are here, where these words were first uttered. I ask for prayers not only for myself but for all pastors, priests, and bishops. Whatever situation we find ourselves in, the important thing is that we see the Lord, point people to him, allow him to direct our catch, and feed and tend the sheep that are his own.

You also have your missions. I hope they will be guided by this same story—recognizing the Lord, building unity, and feeding and tending the flock.

> After this, Jesus revealed himself again to his disciples at the Sea of Tiberias. He revealed himself in this way. Together were Simon Peter, Thomas called Didymus, Nathanael from Cana in Galilee, Zebedee's sons, and two others of his disciples. Simon Peter said to them, "I am going fishing." They said to him, "We also will come with you." So they went out and got into the boat, but that night they caught nothing. When it was already dawn, Jesus was standing on the shore; but the disciples did not realize that it was Jesus. Jesus said to them, "Children, have you caught anything to eat?" They answered him, "No." So he said to them, "Cast the net over the right side of the boat and you will find something." So they cast it, and were not able to pull it in because of the number of fish. So the disciple whom Jesus loved said to Peter, "It is the Lord." When Simon Peter heard that it was the Lord, he tucked in his garment, for he was lightly clad, and jumped into the sea.
>
> —John 21:1-7

Prayer: True Happiness

Loving Father, accept our praise and thanksgiving. We thank You for this beautiful day. We thank You for the promise that this day holds out to us. We thank You for Your loving spirit that will surely work in our minds, in our hearts, and in our community as we continue this spiritual journey.

Today we will hear the echo of Your Son's teaching regarding true happiness and blessedness. The world does not readily accept this teaching. Touch our hearts. May we be the living witnesses to the truth of the Beatitudes, to the quality of our persons, to the quality of our relationships, to the quality of our ethical lives, and to the quality of our community. May people see what true blessedness is.

Dear Father, we thank You for Jesus. We thank You for the Blessed Mother. We thank You for the great men and women of faith who inspire us, who guide us, and who lead us home to You. Accept our thanksgiving in the name of Jesus, in the power of the Holy Spirit, now and forever. Amen.

* Prayer on the way to Mount of Beatitudes.

Day Four

ANATOMY OF A MIRACLE

The event that we are commemorating in this place is a fulfillment of the vision of the prophet Isaiah wherein the times of the Messiah are inaugurated by overflowing food and drink, where hunger is wiped away, and where people can approach God and have their fill. That was the hope of Israel at the time. The fulfillment of the needs of people was associated with the coming of the Messiah. We find such fulfillment in the gospel. We Christians believe that Jesus is the Messiah. In his ministry, in his miracles, we see the prophecies of old being fulfilled. On this very shore of Lake Tiberias, Jesus saw a vast crowd. We are about a hundred here, but there were more than five thousand people then, according to the account. And the miracle of the multiplication of the five barley loaves and two dried fish is something we cannot explain. How did it happen?

Many spiritual writers and commentators try to give us theories, but I don't want to go into that because I don't have a theory.

* Homily at Dalmanutha where Jesus fed thousands of people.

If it's a miracle, then it's a miracle. How it happened? I don't know. If I'm able to explain it, then it may not have been a miracle after all. But we want to look at some elements of the story that will enable us to be, in a way, promoters of miracles too. There are many hungry people, many thirsty people, people whose needs are not met, people who long to come here but cannot. And so we unite ourselves with people who have dreams and whose dreams might end in frustration and despair.

But the story starts within Jesus. It starts with Jesus himself. Seeing the crowds, he felt compassion for them. That's the beginning of the story. A heart that was moved. A heart that is capable of being moved is a heart of flesh. No miracle will happen if the heart of any one of us is a heart of stone.

We need human hearts, hearts of flesh, hearts that will beat for others in pity and compassion. And when the heart is compassionate, it operates on a different level of understanding and reasoning. But then you have the disciples. Jesus tested them. He asked, "Where can we buy enough food for them to eat?" According to St. John's gospel, Jesus knew very well what he intended to do by asking this question. The heart of Philip was revealed. I think all of us can resonate with Philip. He said, "Two hundred days' wages worth of food would not be enough for each of them to have a little!"

Philip's response is not that of a compassionate person. It is the response of a calculating person. He is budget-conscious. If there are five thousand to be fed, how many paychecks would that cost?! But you have more than five thousand. So he was able to calculate quickly—more than two hundred days' wages, and they did not have it. The conclusion then is "let them go home." In another version, the disciples probably wanted to rest but the crowd followed them and Jesus wanted to feed them. Their break time would be disrupted. Imagine feeding five thousand. How can you rest? So they're very calculating: "What about our rest? What about the cost? Where would we get the money to pay for all those?" The conclusion is to forget them and while there is still some light, let them go home and feed themselves.

We can understand that mind-set. It is the prevailing mind-set. It is the mind-set that in a way fosters lack of neighborliness and compassion. In fact, when some of us went to the Marian sites in Europe for the first pilgrimage of JesCom, I was so impressed with the Italian woman who was our guide at Assisi. She was very intelligent. She knew theology. She knew history. She knew the arts. So I asked her at the end whether she was married. She said yes. And I said, "Oh, how many children do you have?" She replied, "Children? With my wages? And my husband's wages? If we had a child we could no longer go on a cruise. No. I'm happy as I am." This is the calculating mentality that makes even children a burden rather than a miracle of life. If you start calculating and calculating, you would not see in a child a miracle; you would only see a burden. And you would exchange the miracle of life for a cruise. The guide even said that they have already saved enough for their next cruise to South America. That may strike us, but if we pause, we realize that in daily life we can be like that too. No one is exempt.

All of us can be tempted to have that mentality. By osmosis, it has become the prevailing mentality. Don't we say all the time that we must be practical? So we end up like Philip and the rest. But Jesus again asserted his mentality. He said, "How much do you have there?" You are so calculating, so I ask how much do you have. Andrew said, "Five barley loaves and two fish." And they added, "But what good are these for so many?" Again, the calculation! But the response of Jesus is, "Have the people recline." Then he took the five loaves and gave thanks to God. He did not calculate. He gave thanks. These meager loaves and fish are gifts from God. Yes, to a calculating mind, this is nothing. But this is everything because it is God's gift, and every gift from God means all, means everything. In the Jewish tradition, the head of the family takes the bread during the meal and gives thanks, recognizing that the bread comes from God. It is God's bread, it is God's gift. Then the father, after giving thanks, realizes that this is no ordinary bread. This is really divine. And if it is a gift, it must continue to be a gift. That's why you break it and pass it on, because if you don't, it loses its being a gift. Thus, the mentality is not so much about calculating things, but looking at everything and everyone as gift.

Try to change the mind-set and your life will change. That's why the great saints come to mind. For example, St. Thérèse of the Child Jesus said that to a blade of grass, everything is grace. Even her sickness was grace. The five loaves and two fish blessed and broken and passed on were more than enough to feed the five thousand.

What also matters is not only the mind-set of Jesus, seeing the world as gift, but also the hands of Jesus. He took the loaves into his hands. There are so many gifts in the world but they fall into the wrong hands. Instead of hands that break and pass on the gifts, sometimes the gifts land in hands that hoard, hands that keep. When you go home after this trip, this pilgrimage, look at your closets. I'm sure you will find things there that you do not need, that you are not using. And your solution is "Let us buy a new closet" or "Let us clear this portion of the room and make new closets." Nothing wrong with your closets, if only you can learn to share. But then, our hands are not the blessed hands. When a pair of blessed hands receives something, that something is a gift which is meant to be given, not hidden. Even in the Philippines, we do not have only five loaves and two pieces of fish. A marine biologist told us that Philippine waters contain the most diverse types of marine life. And if the Philippines could take care of its seas, we could feed the whole world with fish. How bountiful are our blessings! But sadly, if we were to reverse the situation, say five thousand loaves and only five people there, if those five thousand loaves would be handled by a pair of greedy hands, then that number is not enough for five people.

It is not the problem of how many loaves, because there really is enough, even more for everyone. The problem is in the mentality and the hands. Having five loaves of bread and two pieces of fish surely feeds a crowd of five thousand if it is handled by a pair of blessed hands. So check your mentality. To your mind, is everything to be calculated, or do you still have the notion of gift? Let me go to the husbands and wives who have just renewed their marriage vows. How do you look at your spouse? A mouth to feed or a gift? In the family, how do we look at each other? How do we look at children? Are they plus signs to us? Do they add to our income? Or do they diminish our income? Or are they simply gifts? Of course they always say that there is a peso equivalent. Of course, there are fees to pay. But not everything must be measured in terms of money. It is sad, if family members would be keeping count! When married couples bicker they'd say: "Hey you! That electric fan over there, you used my salary to buy that. What about you, you have not bought a single thing for this house!" That is why prenuptial agreements are drawn. They are already calculating when they have not started living together yet. How ironic! They are preparing for a lifetime commitment but they are also preparing for the day of separation. You're already preparing for the demise of the relationship, of the marriage. And even that is calculated. Whereas when you look at it as a gift, then even the problems, even the struggles are part of our growth. They're also gifts, making us strong, making us lively as a couple.

But let me add another element here. Jesus taught the disciples at length. In fact, the preaching came before the miracle of the multiplication of the loaves. That is significant. When Jesus was tempted in the desert, one of the temptations was to turn the stones into bread. What a temptation for a Messiah! If you were the Messiah, you would have liked to share and feed all the people. The temptation was, "Okay, this is quite easy and quick to feed all because a lot of stones are here! You can make enseymada (brioch) or puto (rice bread), or even puto pao (a recipe using rice flour)!" But what did Jesus answer to the devil's temptation? He said, "One does not live by bread alone, but by every word that comes forth from the mouth of God."

That's why, as recounted by Scripture, Jesus gives them the most important bread first: the Word of God. After the Word of God, which is true bread that nourishes and gives us life, he then asks, "Where can we find food, what do you have there?" "Five loaves, two fish." A reminder to all of us, especially to parents and grandparents. This is always something I hear; I heard it from my grandmother. She told my father: "I am a widow. I cannot afford to send you all to schools of your choice because this is all I could afford. I wish that you would send my grandchildren to better schools than where I sent you." That is always the case. We do not like our children or grandchildren to experience the hardships that we went through. But that is okay. We don't want them to suffer much.

But we might give our children a lot of barley loaves and fish, and fail to prepare them for life. They become too comfortable such that when bread is missing, they do not know how to cope. And they do not have the bread of life to sustain them. So some rebel; some just kill themselves. They cannot deal with the absence of the normal bread that we know. That's why it's crucial to give them the bread of life, the Word of God, Jesus himself, especially in the Eucharist. It will unite them with the suffering of Christ and help them find meaning in it, in obedience to the Father and out of compassion for others.

I end with a personal story. I was still a student in the United States when the Tiananmen Square massacre happened in Beijing. There was a young Chinese couple who had gotten out of Beijing, and they were given student visas and scholarships to the Catholic University of America. The wife went into library science and the husband into sociology. I got to know them.

When I finished my doctoral studies in 1992, they invited me to their apartment for dinner. I asked the husband, "Are you enjoying your studies?" He took out the Bible and almost threw it in front of me. He said, "You Catholics, you are wasting your book! This book has profound answers to the search for meaning of the world and human beings. You're wasting it! I've been here for more than three years and no Catholic has invited me to a Bible session, to a Bible reading, to a Bible sharing. No one has invited me. You're very poor in evangelizing." I was tongue-tied because it was true. And also, he fed me dinner, so it was rude to argue.

On my way back, I thought of what he said. Our social ministry is important. We help provide housing, we feed street children, we have a very orderly relief system for victims of calamities, and they are all good and they incarnate the gospel. But we need to give people the bread that is the Word of God. It's not either-or; they must come together. That is why Pope Benedict told the first-world countries, "Okay, you send to the Third World your technology, your so-called expertise, thinking that it will solve the misery of those places. But actually your aid made them poorer. It is what made them the Third World." And then he said, in his typical style, "Oh, we thought, we are giving them bread, but the bread that we sent them turned to stone."

But we don't have to go to the First World. Even among us, without the Word of God, our lives will be lacking. Admittedly, we Catholics suffer in this area, whereas other Christian groups and sects really spend money to spread their interpretation of the word of God. We are more numerous, especially in the Philippines, but why can we not share the Word that gives life?

MESSIAH

Jesus is tempted in the desert. Let us reflect on this special event in the life of Christ, attested to especially by the Synoptic Gospels: St. Matthew, St. Mark, and St. Luke. This occurred after the baptism of Jesus Christ. What a coincidence? Yesterday, we renewed our baptismal vows and now we are here, hopefully driven by the same Holy Spirit that we have received, the way Jesus was driven by the Spirit to the desert to be tempted by the devil.

The temptation of Jesus Christ is pregnant with meaning. The gospel account is replete with symbols. Of course, being tempted, Jesus experiences what all of us, as human beings, experience. Let me clarify, though, that being tempted and sinning are two different things. As a confessor, I hear people confessing not sins, but temptations. Being tempted is not a sin. Giving in to temptation is a sin. What is bad is that it is the subject not the act of giving in to temptation that is being confessed. Wise!

As we've already mentioned, the temptation of Jesus is connected to his baptism. This shows us how he became truly human. He did not separate Himself from us. The human condition became part of his life. This is, in a way, a scandal—to think that God could become so lowly. This seems very un-Godly. It is not fitting of God. But this is how much God loves us. He became human so that God could redeem even the shameful, the embarrassing parts of our human existence. At the same time, Jesus here is a symbol. He fasted for forty days and forty nights and was tempted by the devil. Jesus here is the symbol of the old Israel that wandered in the desert for forty years. This was

* Talk given at Mount of Temptations in the city of Jericho.

the Israelites' preparation for entering the Promised Land, for becoming a covenanted people.

Yet, in the desert for forty years, Israel also was tempted. There were many people who complained while in the desert. Some of them even said, "Let us just go back to Egypt." The basic temptation is that you are already being led by God, yet you miss the food in Egypt. You miss the comforts in Egypt. And so you say "Better to go back to *slavery!*" They were so greedy. They would rather go back to slavery as long as there was food to eat. And so Jesus here experiences what Israel experienced before, but the outcome will be different. If the old Israel succumbed to temptations, here Jesus, the beginning of the new Israel, the new people in the covenant of his blood, will come out triumphant.

But there is another concern here. The temptations that Jesus underwent were temptations about who God is. *Who is really God?* The temptation was also very unique to Jesus because it concerned what type of messiah and what type of messiahship he would embrace. Let us keep those things in mind.

In this sense, Jesus can also be considered the new Elijah. Remember how at Carmel we reflected on how Elijah fought for the true God. Here Jesus, the new Elijah, will proclaim first to the devil who God truly is. He will also fight for the plan of God, which is very different from the plans that we have or make in our daily lives. With all that as a background, let us go briefly through the three temptations.

The first temptation is to turn the stones into bread. The temptation is to be a Messiah that is a magician, a Messiah that has powers and thus can do everything and save humanity without any effort. This is the traditional (even contemporary) mind-set of cutting corners. In class, if one would have the chance to cheat, he'd cheat. That is easier than having to study. Money is quicker to earn if one sells drugs rather than work an honest day-to-day job. Cut corners! Find the easier way to achieve salvation. And the devil knew just how to tempt the Son of God. Look at the beginning of the temptation: If You are truly the Son of God, then use Your power. Command these stones to turn into bread. So Jesus is being tempted to prove that he is truly the Son of God.

And he is asked to prove that by showing his magical powers. Aside from the temptation to cut corners, we also experience the temptation to prove ourselves. That is scary. Sometimes, we do a lot of things just for self-glory.

One personal example: Why will I prepare my homilies? My motivation, I hope, is so that I can be true to the Word of God and I can nurture people. But it can be that I will craft my homilies well in order to prove my eloquence, in order to prove to people that I am a cut above the rest. "If you are Chito . . . if you are the bishop!" That's a temptation. So you try to do things well, not because they merit your self-giving but because you want to prove to the world who you are. To you married couples, there is no need to prove anything. Just love your spouse. Love is not a matter of proving myself, my worth, but of serving the other, my beloved, my spouse. Parents also try to prove themselves to their children. Or the children try to prove themselves as worthy children of their parents. There's no need for that. Do everything with purity of intention—love. You have a mission. Do it well because you are convinced of it and not because you want to prove who "I am" and use the mission to gain adulation and a good self-image. When that happens, it is no longer service but self-service, serving the self.

But the Messiah was not sent by the Father to prove himself. He came to save. So his focus is on others, not on himself. A messiah who is here in order to be hailed as one and who will do everything and anything to gain that recognition loses his focus. It's no longer the good of others but his own good. This then is the first temptation, and the response of Jesus is, "One does not live by bread alone, but by every word that comes forth from the mouth of God." So we need to be nurtured by the Word of God, we need to be purified by the Word of God.

Now the second temptation. Jesus was taken to the parapet of the temple and was told to jump. To jump because the Bible says, "He will command his angels . . . and with their hands they will support you." Here the temptation is to test God. If the first temptation is to prove yourself to be the Son of God, now it is for you to challenge God. Something like, "God, show me that You are true to Your Word." But Jesus tells the devil, "You shall not put the Lord, your God, to the test." There are many ways by which we put God to the test. The most subtle way is to make God fit our plans, our mentality, our programs, and our dreams. Like, for example, "Lord, I have a good plan that I like. And because it is a good plan I want you to let it happen. If you don't, well, then what kind of God are you?" That's very subtle. Indeed, most of the time we pray for really noble and good things—our desires for our families, for our children, for our friends, for our nation, for the church. They're all good, and we want God to agree with our plans. Now this is very subtle. Of course, in prayer, we are free to express our heart's desires to God. It is priceless, but we have to be careful. It starts with goodness, but the devil is quick to enter. Sometimes, we think we are praying, when in truth, we are not. We're already testing God.

I'll give you a very dramatic example. I know this does not happen every day. I met a guy who's very active in church. He already had four daughters, but still he continuously prayed: "I hope that I could have a son." There is nothing wrong in asking for that in the prayer. But he told me, "Father, I already have four daughters." His wife is heavy with child. "If this baby is not a boy, I am leaving the church. What kind of God is he if he cannot grant me the son for whom I ask?" I kidded him. "Oh, c'mon, whether a girl or a boy, you already have five. You are blessed!

As for us (clergy) we don't even have one, and you—you've already got five!" How ridiculous! Some couples are praying for children, and then they accept the will of God. But this man has been blessed with children but he looked at them not as his own, not like human beings. He vowed to leave the church if his newborn was a girl. (Incidentally, the newborn was a girl!) And so he left the church and dragged his own family with him. He used to be a lay eucharistic minister, and his wife used to be a volunteer catechist. They left the church. As I said, this is a dramatic example of putting God to the test. I know we don't do it that way every day, but let us be warned. It may not come to us in such a glaring manner or fashion but we are putting God to the test when the infinite God is being forced into our finite, limited plans. Very often, we force the infinite God to fit into our worldly limited plans, giving him ultimatums like, for instance, "Lord, that is strike one already!"

The relationship is reversed. "Who is really the true God—you or Him?" Why do we expect God to obey us, yet we do not expect ourselves to obey God? Who is really the true God? As I said, the temptation of Jesus is really about who is God, and many times we pretend to be God. In our relationship with God, we replace Him, subvert Him, subordinate Him. In one of the episodes of *The Word Exposed*, the reading was about forgiveness. That was the Word of God: forgive. A viewer sent an e-mail: "Dear Bishop Chito, was Jesus really serious when He said that? I have a brother who did me harm. How can I forgive him? I'm sure Jesus has room for exceptions." The one who sent it to me wanted me to revise the next episode to correct what I said about forgiveness. But who am I to change the Word of God? Who am I to challenge God? I myself find it difficult. All of us find it hard to forgive. But God has spoken. Do we challenge Him? Or will His word challenge us? Why are we reversing or subverting the relationship?

At this point we can recall the times when we wanted God to be our obedient slave and to be a God according to our plans and our image and likeness, instead of us being formed always according to His plans and according to His image and likeness.

The third temptation. Jesus was taken to a very high mountain and the devil showed him all the kingdoms of the world in their magnificence and said, "All these I shall give to you, if you will prostrate yourself and worship me." There you are—a change of gods! The devil became very blunt. "I am now your god, worship me." In return for that change of God, or change of the object of worship, you will gain everything! That is, everything in this world, the kingdoms of this world.

In Barcelona a favorite tourist spot is a mountain named *Tibidabo*. That's Latin: *tibi*, "to you," + *dabo*, "I will give." Precisely the words from the gospel: "I will give to you all the kingdoms." Because on that mountain, you see the whole of Barcelona, all the kingdoms promised to you. But this temptation happens. People can easily change gods. And this does not happen in a dramatic manner where I renounce my religion. I may be exteriorly very religious. All the novena prayer books, different kinds of rosaries, and assorted pieces of relics are in my bag, which I always carry with me. I can be exteriorly Catholic, pious Catholic. But there is such a thing as a practical atheist. Religiously I am a believer, but practically I am an atheist.

If I review my life, I ask myself: To whom do I render worship and service? That is my God! And to that God I will offer sacrifice. I will even sacrifice myself for that God.

I talked about this during the 2008 International Eucharistic Congress in Quebec and was surprised when people started clapping. Perhaps it hit them too. I mentioned then that for the God called profit, we have many worshippers. Many people worship profit and they will sacrifice neighbors, they will sacrifice human beings in order to worship profit. Some worship the false god of pleasure; they engage in what is called hedonism. For their self-pleasure, they will sacrifice so many values and even human beings. How many women have been sacrificed to sex tourism and slavery? When we go around Asia, this is one big problem, the abuse of what they call "the girl child."

In Thailand I once attended a meeting, part of which was an interview with a girl, a teenager sold by her own father to prostitution. When the father was interviewed, he pointed to a house, saying, "Had I not sold my daughter to prostitution, I could not have bought that house." And the daughter, when she was interviewed, said the same thing: "We needed a house, so it was all okay." At the time of the interview, there was suspicion that she had AIDS. How sad! For a house, you sacrifice your daughter. At another meeting, we were told that some businessmen would offer their wives to their business partners to seal a deal. "O, dress well. Doll up yourself. We'll have dinner tonight with a foreign investor. And, after dinner, you-know-what will happen." My God! So the business is their god to whom they sacrifice their wives!

The mountain of temptation is found everywhere where the true God is challenged, where the true God is replaced, where true worship that only God deserves is misplaced, where the true Messiah is being tempted not to be the humble servant of God, where pride, self-focus, becomes the invitation. Thanks be to God these temptations were overcome by Jesus. And so we learn from Jesus how to fight temptations. Yes, the devil used the Word of God, but he distorted it. What did Jesus do? His main tool in fighting temptation was the very Word of God.

We have to admit, though, that we are poor in evangelism. We are poor in the Word of God, even if it is our weapon against temptation. Remember the wedding at Cana. Mary told Jesus there was no more wine. Then Jesus said, "Woman, what is that to me?" Humbly, she said, "Just do what he tells you." Ever since I became a bishop, many people have approached my mother,

"Tell Bishop to be the presider of my child's wedding. Tell Bishop to do the blessing of my house." How do I fight off these overwhelming requests? I use the Word of God. I tell my mother: "Woman, what is that to me? My time has not yet come. I have no time." And she goes to the neighbors and says, "Do whatever he tells you. If he says no, then it's no." Use the Word of God. If you are tempted to be proud, use the Word of God. The Lord is my light and my salvation, not myself.

For every situation in life, have the Word handy. Rely not on your own word. Our words are not strong enough to fight off the devil. So use the Word of God. If we say: "Later on, devil. Come back later." It will surely revisit. A human word. But the Word of God is "Get behind me, Satan!" So, not my word, but the Word of God. Use it. But how can we use the Word of God if we do not know the Word of God?

At one catechetical gathering a catechist shared, "I teach my students that Jesus said, 'Cleanliness is next to godliness.'" Really? Did Jesus say that? Know the Word of God, the power of the Word of God.

Jesus showed something else: determination. He was not wishy-washy. According to St. Ignatius in his rules of discernment, the devil rejoices when he sees the one being tempted panicking or rattled. So, in the face of temptation, be firm. Do not be like "on the one hand, but on the other hand, or maybe this, or maybe that. . . ." You will be tempted. Ignatius tells us further that the tempter is like a pesky child. The more you entertain this child, the more he will annoy you. So ignore with finality. Be firm. Every New Year we make many resolutions. I will exercise three times a week. I will lose weight, but then you go to a feast and forget about your resolutions. We cannot say no with finality.

My final point: Jesus was clear about his mission. He knew what type of Messiah the Lord wanted him to be. With clarity of vision, just ward off everything that is against that vision, and make your life simple. Make your life simple. There are many things that can distort your vision or mission. For example, the mission of teachers is to teach. But there are teachers who would be selling wares or food during recess. What are you—a peddler or a teacher? Be clear! If you are a teacher, then be a teacher; a spouse, be a spouse. If you are a priest, then be a priest. Not like a priest in the morning, but when evening comes, he'd transform into another personality. That is temptation.

So we have to be clear about our mission and our identity emerging from that mission. Jesus is our inspiration. We are consoled by the fact that Jesus, who is the new Israel, the new Elijah, got out of the desert, got out of the wilderness whole and intact. He did it not only for himself but for all of us, giving us the courage and the grace to fight the devil, the evil one.

Let us therefore encourage one another to cling to the Word of God. Let us strive to be firm about our faith so that when we encounter the devil in the many deserts of our lives, we will know how to handle him.

Mary's Song of Praise

And Mary said:
"My soul proclaims the greatness of the Lord;
  my spirit rejoices in God my savior.
For he has looked upon his handmaid's lowliness;
  behold, from now on will all ages call me blessed.
The Mighty One has done great things for me,
  and holy is his name.
His mercy is from age to age
  to those who fear him.
He has shown might with his arm,
  dispersed the arrogant of mind and heart.
He has thrown down the rulers from their thrones
  but lifted up the lowly.
The hungry he has filled with good things;
  the rich he has sent away empty.
He has helped Israel his servant,
  remembering his mercy,
according to his promise to our fathers,
  to Abraham and to his descendants forever."

—Luke 1:46-55

Day Five

PREGNANT

Some points for reflection. First, when a woman is pregnant, she is supposed to be filled with the Holy Spirit. This is something we need to recover. Instead of thinking about ripe mango that tastes like guava. When you are bearing life within you, it is the Spirit that is at work, and every word that is uttered is a prophecy in praise of God. So let us remind families expecting children that these are moments to be prophets, to be filled with the life-giving Spirit.

Second, Elizabeth was able to pinpoint how Mary became a mother. She said, "Blessed are you who believed that what was spoken to you by the Lord would be fulfilled." Elizabeth was given the inspiration by the Holy Spirit to understand that the motherhood of Mary was not an act of human relationships but an act of the Spirit, and the response is faith. So parents must understand that they may be biological parents, but they

* Talk given at the Church of the Visitation, Jerusalem.

are also responsible for the transmission of the life of faith to their children.

Those two should come together. I don't only transmit biological life. In the tradition of the Jews, true life is found in our relationship with God. Even if I'm biologically okay, if my relationship with God is not all right, then I'm actually dead. So parents transmit two types of life—one is the biological and the other one is life in God. It's not enough that I provide my children food, clothing, shelter, or education. How about faith?

A final point about Mary. When she was greeted by Elizabeth, Mary could have bragged. She could have said, "Sorry, Elizabeth, I am the chosen one, not you. I am more special." No. She said, "My soul proclaims the greatness of the Lord." She saw that it was the hand of God, the gracious God, that did this miracle in her. There's no reason to be proud; everything is God's work. And because Mary was humble, she associated herself with the humble people of Israel. What she experienced as God's graciousness, she hoped would be experienced by the poor of Israel, the hungry, and the lowly. As if she was expressing, "God looks upon me, the lowly, with mercy. Therefore you, you will never go hungry for he will feed you; he will lift up the meek and lowly. I feel for you." Despite her stature, she did not distance herself from the general population. But we, even if we were the barangay captains only, gosh, we think as if we were somebody.

Even the barangay captain's wife bears an attitude of self-importance and disassociates herself from the "common people." And then we don't feel poor people anymore. The Magnificat of Mary is a prophetic sign that whenever you are graced you should not forget God and you should not forget the lowly. Please, whenever you are graced, never forget God and never forget the little ones. That is the best way to praise God.

CHRISTMAS

Let me start my sharing by reminding you that you still have to attend Mass on December 25. Some of you might not show up in church in your parishes for Christmas Eve Mass or Christmas Day Mass because you've already celebrated Christmas right here in Bethlehem. Indeed this is a privilege. We can share with our families or our communities this privileged experience of coming here, to that original place where the angels proclaimed to the shepherds the Good News that the Savior had been born. But do it humbly. That is the spirit of Bethlehem, this lowly humble town not realizing that in its littleness that it would make and change history.

As a priest, I find preparing a homily for Christmas quite exciting. At the same time, it can be confusing because of the many possible meanings and symbols you can dwell on, so the great temptation is to cover everything. Instead of giving a homily, you might end up giving a convention. But let us focus on a few things; we don't need to cover everything. Here in the City of David, all those who belonged to the tribe of David had to come to fulfill the order of Caesar Augustus that a census, an enrollment, be held. And since Joseph belonged to the line of David, he had to come here in order to be registered with his wife who at the time was with child. This is the place, the very City of David, that became the birthplace of this child, who was enveloped in a lot of mystery.

Try to imagine Mary here more than two thousand years ago. Try to imagine Joseph. If you were Joseph, what would you think of when Mary starts experiencing labor pains? If you were Mary,

* Homily at Mass held at the Church of St. Catherine, Bethlehem.

what would cross your mind? Remember that her pregnancy was clouded by mystery. In fact, we can even say, it was an anomalous pregnancy. If I were Joseph and saw that Mary was in labor, I would surely say, "This is it! This is what the angel told me. What could this be? Is this a human being? My wife is pregnant even if nothing is consummated. Yet I have faith. But what kind of creature will this be?" Mary herself did not understand everything so she was probably excited, full of anticipation and at the same time anxiety. "What will this child be?"

People asked the same question when John the Baptist was born because he was another example of an anomalous birth—a mother who was barren and a father who was very old. Without God's intervention, no John the Baptist could have come, It was the same with Jesus. Based on norms, these two births, intimately connected, are out of this world. But the identity of the child is the object of the revelation. The angels appeared to the shepherds in the field, and to these lowly shepherds was announced the news that the people of Israel had been waiting for. That was the object of the first reading from Isaiah, a time of peace, a time of restoration, a time of unity. No more war, no more sorrow, no more anger. Only love, only oneness. According to Isaiah, it will happen because a child will be born to us, and the angels announced to the shepherds the fulfillment of this long-standing dream.

The sign that the Savior is born is worth reflecting on. You would think that if the one being born is a savior, then it should be in a setting befitting a savior: the best delivery room in a hospital, the top doctors, a gold or at least gilded crib. Everything must be pure and immaculate. Instead, we are told, the sign that the Savior is born is that a baby in swaddling clothes would be lying in a lowly manger, truly a child, truly poor. Cardinal Henry Newman, reflecting on Christmas while looking at the baby, exclaimed, "omnipotence in bonds." The omnipotent God is now tied in swaddling clothes. The Creator is now a lowly creature, the owner of the earth is now to be born. Almighty God has truly become a child, and it is the way of childhood that will save the world. It is the way of childhood, poverty, dependence on God that will change the world. This is clear, and human history testifies that there is no peace, there is no salvation, there is no unity when pride reigns, when people want to dominate one another, when there is no childlike purity, when there is no recognition of God, when we play God, when we graduate from being children and pretend that we can handle everything and run everything. No salvation will come in this context.

That's why later on Jesus will say, "Unless you turn and become like children, you will not enter the kingdom of heaven." Be a child! But of course our world teaches us different ways of being children. There's the cosmetic way. Having a facelift surgery, procedures of cut-and-tuck here and there can deceive one to believe that he or she is actually young and youthful again. The bald would have hair transplants, while those with hair dye it with any assorted colors believing that it would make them feel and look younger. That is not the childlikeness the baby in the manger teaches us. Seriously, some who look like seventy-year-olds act and talk like someone much younger, fantasizing that they actually look youthful when truthfully they just appear odd. The world is teaching us a different type of being a child, or childlikeness.

Let us go back to Bethlehem, where being a child is being helpless even if you are the Creator, even if you owned everything. You become a lowly creature and in the end helpless to be able to say, "I need God." Do I really need God? Christmas is coming. Train your husband or wife or your children to give as Christmas gift Jesus himself. "What gift do you have for me this time?" "I have one—it is Jesus!" I am sure your children would resent you for that. But He is what we need.

So do we really need the Savior? Sadly, the celebration of Christmas has become defocused. It is no longer the birth of the Savior who showed us the path of salvation that becomes the focus. Christmas has become heavily commercial. It has become cute. It has become all about calories and food, all about feasting without Jesus the child. That's why I encourage you, during the Christmas season, to have a crib or *belen* in your house. You may forgo Rudolph the reindeer and Santa Claus as long as you have Jesus, Mary, Joseph, and the shepherds. It is a catechetical moment when people gather there, and we are made one by Jesus, the lowly child.

The other lesson is Bethlehem. One of the prophecies told about Bethlehem goes something like "Oh, you are a negligible town. You are not the greatest of towns. But from you will come the Savior." Even the choice of the place of the Savior's birth follows the pedagogy of lowliness and of being a child.

In 1997 I was appointed by Pope John Paul II to the Vatican's International Theological Commission, a group of twenty-eight theologians from all over the world. Our boss at the time was Cardinal Joseph Ratzinger, the future pope. On the first day of the meeting we were asked to introduce ourselves. I was at the end of the line. Each one said, "I'm Professor So-and-so from Naples, Italy, or from Strasbourg, or Budapest." I was the last, and I said, "I'm Professor Tagle from Imus." They asked, "Where is that?" I said to myself, "My hometown, my place of origin is the only one that they have not heard of." I became an exotic item for them. "Imus? Where is Imus?" But I showed them what a person from Imus and the Philippines could give. I was the youngest at the time.

I remember telling myself then, "Just be a child in the midst of these serious theologians." So every time I opened my mouth they would laugh. That was my role. I just made them laugh. At the Synod of Bishops in Rome last November, as we were being introduced, Cardinal Lavada, who took the place of Cardinal Ratzinger, exclaimed, "Oh, Bishop Tagle, how is Imus?" Wow, they know now! And so the other bishops were teasing me, "Why do they know only of your diocese?" I replied, "Because they amusingly laughed at me before, so until now, they could not forget me." But it feels good. It feels good that you don't brag about yourself, you don't brag about your simple town. When we were in Nazareth that was also the question: "Can anything good come from Nazareth?" Can anything good come from Imus? Can anything good come from Sorsogon or from Naga or from Cabanatuan? "Can anything good come from Bethlehem?" In these lowly places God comes with all His power and might but in the form of a lowly child. So let us remember our own "Bethlehems" and see how in the humility, in the humble beginnings of our places of origin, our families, God can do a lot of good, but only if we follow the path of the child born in the manger. So be a lowly child, be light, be a bringer of peace in the world.

Let us now pause and open our hearts to the light of the child, the babe born in Bethlehem. May His light drive away all pretension, all pride, all false sense of grandeur. May we remain humble and poor, relying only on the light that comes from God.

Prayer: Shepherds

'Twas revealed for the very first time that the Messiah had been born.

Loving Father, we thank you for choosing lowly people, people not recognized by the world, to be the bearers of your Good News. In union with the shepherds and poor people of the world, we offer you

* Prayer at shepherds' fields, Bethlehem.

our praise, our thanksgiving, and our supplications. After each petition we shall say,

"Lord, hear our prayer."

We pray for government officials, who are civil shepherds. May they be poor in spirit. May pride not take the better of them like the poor shepherds in Bethlehem. May all government officials be bearers of the Good News and may they be men and women of prayer, seeing angels and hearing messages from God. Let us pray to the Lord.

Lord, hear our prayer.

We pray for shepherds in the military, they who are supposed to guarantee the safety of nations and peoples the way the shepherds did at the time of Jesus for their sheep. May self-interest be taken away from their minds and hearts. May ambition be replaced by genuine concern for the people they are asked to serve and protect. Let us pray to the Lord.

Lord, hear our prayer.

We pray for shepherds in the families—parents, grandparents, guardians. May they be solicitous of their children, grandchildren, and those that the Lord has given them to take care of, to nurture, and to animate. May the parents who are encountering difficulties with their children learn the ways of shepherding according to the ways of Jesus. Let us pray to the Lord.

Lord, hear our prayer.

We pray for shepherds in the education sector. May all educators take to heart their responsibility of leading tender lambs and sheep to the true waters of wisdom. May they lead them to the real pasture of values, of virtues, of the fear of God. Let us pray to the Lord.

Lord, hear our prayer.

We pray for shepherds in the arts, sciences, and social communication. May they realize that what they are doing is not just work and not just producing shows and programs for people to support. May they realize that through their ministry, through their work, they are shaping minds and hearts, especially of the young. May they be responsible and accountable to God. Let us pray to the Lord.

Lord, hear our prayer.

For the shepherds in the church—whether ordained, religious, or lay—may we all learn from Jesus, the Good Shepherd. May we open ourselves to his love, his selflessness, and his willingness to lay down his life for his sheep. May every shepherd in the church be a mirror of Jesus, the one sent by the Father to shepherd us to his kingdom. Let us pray to the Lord.

Lord, hear our prayer.

And we pray for the sheep who are lost, confused, infirm, wounded, and waiting for shepherds to come to them, to carry them home. We remember those who are abandoned, those who feel alone, those whom society would rather forget. May the Lord send them shepherds to show them his compassion, love and concern. Let us pray to the Lord.

Lord, hear our prayer.

In silence let us now pray for our own intentions.

Lord, hear our prayer.

Day Six

SORROW

We have been following the steps of Jesus leading to this sacred place, where the whole drama of our salvation is worked out, not in an exteriorly dramatic manner but more in the heart of Jesus. The exterior drama will happen at Calvary but here we find Jesus in prayer. He and his disciples have just come from the Passover meal where as a community of disciples they prayed together. Here Jesus prayed alone but he brought his three closest friends to stay at a distance from him while he prayed. The quality of Jesus' prayer should be the model for all of us, especially in moments of agony and struggle. How do we pray? First, the quality of Jesus' sorrow. We have gone to Dominus Flevit where Jesus wept. Here Jesus would say his soul was so distressed, and in the version of St. Matthew he says, "My soul is overwhelmed with sorrow to the point of death." He could have died here, already, of sorrow. It is clear in the gospels that Jesus wept not

* Homily at Mass offered in the Church of All Nations (or Church of the Agony), Jerusalem.

for himself but because Jerusalem failed to recognize the moment of his visitation.

Jerusalem was so blessed with prophets and now by the visitation of the Son of God. But Jerusalem missed out on it, and for that Jesus weeps for Jerusalem. Here we reflect on his sorrow. We can ask ourselves: What do we weep for? What are the causes of our sorrows? Are they similar to the tears of Christ? Jesus wept on account of mission, on account of God being rejected by people. Admittedly, many times our tears are self-centered. We cry because we do not get what we want, our plans do not proceed according to our desires. Young people even kill themselves because they do not get what they want from their parents. Oh, our sorrows are cute. Some people don't even talk with one another because of one piece of chocolate candy that was not given to them when they were in nursery school, and after fifty years they have not forgiven. How self-centered! Let us therefore ask that we may weep for others and for God. That makes our sorrows Christian; that makes our sorrows redemptive.

The second point is the very prayer of Jesus here. It was the prayer of a Son who was suddenly enveloped by fear and terror. Some people say that the agony in the garden was make-believe. They say, "Oh, after all, Jesus is the Son of God, he knows that he'll resurrect from the dead. So His fear is not true, it is a show." No! He is truly human and so his fear is also real. Who will not tremble before the forces of evil, conniving to kill you? Who will not tremble before death, looming before your very eyes? Who will not tremble? We sinful human beings tremble a lot. I trembled this morning when we were told to guard our wallets and purses. I trembled and said, "Wow, even in the holiest of places, you find dangers." We sinful human beings tremble before evil; we tremble before death.

But Jesus is life, the author of life. How can the author of life not be fearful before the very enemy of life? Jesus is all goodness. He is purity itself. How can goodness not tremble before its enemy, evil? The closest that I can give as an example happened when I was a seminarian. The rector was Fr. Eduardo Hontiveros, the great musician, and one member of the faculty was Fr. Ruben Tanseco, who was a concert pianist. At morning Mass our voices—my classmates' and mine—usually cracked and could not reach the high notes. These two priests would call our attention and say, "Oh, you seminarians, why are you mangling, destroying the songs?" But we did not think that we were destroying the songs; we just thought that we were singing. Father Tanseco would add, "My fine ears are suffering." The musicians suffer before the opposite. We do not.

My mother is from Pangasinan, so she is used to eating *pinakbet* cooked in clay pots. When we are invited to homes and served *pinakbet*, she tastes it and whispers to me, "They used the stainless steel pot for this, not the clay pot, which is better!" "Mother, keep quiet; we are guests here." She suffers; I do not. Here, Jesus suffered. We no longer suffer before evil and death. Why? Maybe because we are already on the side of evil and death? The human part of Jesus said, "Let this cup pass from me. I do not want to experience the horror of evil and death, which are very much against who I am." But in the end, the human will of Jesus gave way to the will of the Son. "Not as I will, but as you will."

This is how we are saved. This is how the Son of God worked out the drama of our salvation. He assumed and embraced into his heart whatever was against him, even terror, evil, injustice, betrayal. He transformed everything into love, the love of the Son for the Father and the love of neighbor for others. And his love is greater than all the sins and evil and injustice that he allowed to enter into his heart. Lamb of God, you take away the sins of the world.

Let me close with a beautiful line from the document produced by the Asian bishops at our meeting on the Eucharist.

Reflecting on the Last Supper and the Agony in the Garden, the document talks about how Jesus turned the night of betrayal into a dawn of hope by his love. Summing up, let us reflect on the quality of our sorrows. Let us reflect on the quality of our prayer. We pray that our human will, by the grace of God, may be transformed into the will of the children of God. Because when that happens, like Jesus in the agony in the garden, we see strength, we see hope. He says, "Get up, let us go. Look, my betrayer is at hand." He can now face his mission.

This is a place of prayer. Those of you who are struggling with your mission in life, those of you who have sorrows you want purified, this is the place to pray, and let the prayer of Jesus be ours too.

THE MISSION CONTINUES

He became human. He became flesh. He descended from the Father to us and here fulfilled his mission, his mission of love, his mission of healing, his mission of peace. Not everything turned out well for Jesus. This mission of love took its culmination, its culminating point, in his death, his dying for love and dying as the greatest lover of God and of humanity.

Now, in his resurrection and ascension into heaven, we see God saying a very loud "Yes" to this person whom his enemies

* Talk at the Church of the Ascension, Jerusalem.

considered a failure. The world said "No" to Jesus; the Father says, "Yes, this is truly my Son and I take him back to me. He came from me, now He returns to me." The ascension is the entry of Jesus again into the very life of God. That does not mean he is not present among us. But being present in the Father, being seated at the right hand of the Father, he is very much present to us, but in a different way. That's why we can say, "You who are seated at the right hand of the Father, receive our prayer."

The ascension is the continuation of Jesus' mission. He does not stop praying for us. He does not stop looking at our concerns, responding to our needs, but now he does so as a brother in the presence of God. *Let's say that you have a fellow town mate that suddenly has been appointed assistant personnel at Malacañang.** My, it is as if having a "man" in there that is "seated at the right hand of the father." You feel good that you have an inside connection. Jesus, our brother, is in God's presence, the true God that came down to become a human being. Could God the Almighty ever leave us? But do we thank God for this dignity, this beautiful grace granted to us in the ascension of Jesus? But let me close by saying, the angels told the apostles, "Why are you looking up?" Why are you all looking up? He is coming down again.

Jesus is coming back. Jesus goes to heaven but we're left here on earth. He completed His mission; now our mission begins.

Jesus ascends to heaven. That is the fulfillment of his mission. He now goes to the One who sent him to report, and the One who sent him really gave him more than a passing mark. He was given a Name above any other name. But we remain here. So the mission that we have received from Jesus, now we perform. From this Mount of Olives, the disciples would go to the ends of the earth proclaiming Jesus. Hopefully, we let the mark of the

* Malacañang is the Philippine equivalent of the White House or 10 Downing Street.

foot of Jesus remind us: We have to walk and leave his footprints in our homes, in our families, wherever we go so that his Name may be glorified.

After the sabbath, as the first day of the week was dawning, Mary Magdalene and the other Mary came to see the tomb. And behold, there was a great earthquake; for an angel of the Lord descended from heaven, approached, rolled back the stone, and sat upon it. His appearance was like lightning and his clothing was white as snow. The guards were shaken with fear of him and became like dead men. Then the angel said to the women in reply, "Do not be afraid! I know that you are seeking Jesus the crucified. He is not here, for he has been raised just as he said. Come and see the place where he lay. Then go quickly and tell his disciples, 'He has been raised from the dead, and he is going before you to Galilee; there you will see him.' Behold, I have told you."

—Matthew 28:1-7

Day Seven

BEARERS OF LIGHT

Alleluia! We're celebrating in this church the mystery of the resurrection of the Lord. We believe, coming here to the sacred sites, that the resurrection truly happened. We can even point to the tomb where Jesus was buried, the tomb that was discovered to be empty. The event of the resurrection happened in history and changed it. At the same time, from the gospel accounts we realize that the resurrection is also an event beyond history. It cannot be fully understood and explained if we rely on merely human historical and time-bound categories. That's why the account in St. Matthew uses the images of earthquake, of stones being rolled, of angels speaking. All these tell us that this event, while truly historical, is also beyond history. It is transcendent. Eternity meets history. Pure divinity now comes to humanity.

I want to start my reflection by borrowing an idea from Pope Benedict XVI. In his latest book on Jesus, he writes that the resurrection of Jesus is something like this: Jesus is, of course,

* Homily at the Latrun Monastery.

truly God but he became truly human to carry out a mission. He worked as a human being and died as a human being, but in his resurrection he entered into the realm of God, the very life of God.

There is a difference between resurrection and resuscitation. When you are resuscitated, you come back to life, that is, to the same life you had before. For example, you drowned. You received help and were resuscitated when you drowned. You came back to life, the life that you had. Then it is back to toiling and working, feeling the pangs of hunger, encountering temptations, and sadden with frustrations. You are back to your earthly life. But the resurrection of Christ was not a resuscitation, a return to life as usual here on earth. When he rose from the dead, he found life in God. The life that he now lives is God's life. And, in the realm of God, there is no more sorrow, no more sin, no more death, only life. In the resurrection, God has made the space in the life of God for one human being, who is the head of the church, and with him, there is space for all of us. Jesus himself told us that "In my Father's house there are many dwelling places. If there were not, would I have told you that I am going to prepare a place for you?"

So, rising from the dead, the true resurrection, means that after death I experience life, but not the life that I have been used to, but life in God. No wonder, then, that Jesus the risen One, fully alive with the life of God, could enter rooms that were locked. He could just appear in the midst of people. His body is different. He was not even recognized because his humanity was now filled with the life of God, the light of God. That is our hope.

Just like now as we are on pilgrimage, we pray, we cry, and we feel as if we are so close to God. Every day we pray and hear Mass. Jesus is always in our thoughts and we feel difference and change in our lives. With that new aura, you will not be easily recognized when you go home. Your spouse would say, "Is that you? You look different." Your children would ask, "Daddy, Mommy, is that you? You seem different." After attending a retreat and receiving a deep religious experience, you change and feel different. Imagine, we are not yet experiencing the real resurrection.

I remember when I first saw Mother Teresa of Calcutta. The woman simply exuded holiness. You could see the difference. But this is our hope: the final transformation where our life here on earth will be given a space in God's life and there will be a new heaven and a new earth, where all tears will be wiped away and all fears will be gone.

But we need to enter the experience of Mary of Magdala and the other Mary at the tomb. They witnessed this spiritually frightening event and they did not recognize Jesus the first time. And look at the guards who were placed there to make sure that his body would not be stolen, that the resurrection would not happen. According to the gospel, after an earthquake the angel descended and the stone was rolled back. The guards were paralyzed by fear of him and fell down like dead men.

At the resurrection of Christ to new life, those who were against him looked dead. Those who wanted him dead could not stand his life. Those who wanted Him in the darkness of the tomb could not stand his light. It was fearful, but then the reassuring words of the angel: "He has been raised from the dead, and he is going before you to Galilee; there you will see him."

We are coming to the close of our pilgrimage, and the same words of Jesus to the women should ring true in our ears and our hearts: "Do not be afraid. Go and carry the news to my brothers and sisters that they are to go to Galilee where they will see me." Seeing the risen Lord involves a mission. To see the risen Lord is to be changed into the bearer of the Good News that we have seen Him and that He is there going ahead of us to meet other men and women.

The privilege of having joined the pilgrimage should lead to the Christian responsibility and obligation of mission. Don't go home and brag about your trip just to make others jealous: "You should have gone with us. It was amazing. Here, here is the handkerchief that I wiped it with. No, don't touch it, this is for me alone. I wiped this on the sacred fixture, but I do not like it to lose its power. This is for my use only." Gosh, its "effectiveness" or "power" would truly go away.

Every privilege carries with it a responsibility.

It is not by chance that we as a community have been brought by the Lord here to encounter him, to experience his light. Like the first women who witnessed him, we can go without fear to carry the news. Jesus is real and he is out there to meet everyone. Here is a beautiful description of the manner on how the women walked away. Half overjoyed, half fearful, they ran to carry the Good News. The feelings of joy and fear were intertwined. Joy because Jesus was alive, yet fear because it was different, it was not an ordinary situation. Who would believe them? But with joy and fear they ran. They ran. So later, at the closing of the Mass, when the priest says "Go in peace," you will run like Mary of Magdala and the other woman with utter eagerness—the right foot eager, the left foot overjoyed, but running just the same, as bearers of the light of Christ, *Lumen Christi*. As the prophet says, "The people walking in darkness have seen a great light." May the sparks of the light of Christ be ours and may we kindle that spark even years after our pilgrimage. Remember the graces received here, but also remember that the privilege of a pilgrimage carries with it a missionary responsibility.